Towards Speculative Realism

Essays and Lectures

T0033905

CONTENTS

Preface

This volume assembles eleven previously unpublished essays and lectures written between 1997 and 2009. A great deal happened between those two dates. In 1997 I was an obscure doctoral student at DePaul University in Chicago in the midst of a sportswriting career. Although my novel interpretation of Heidegger was exciting to many fellow students, there was nothing more to my credit than that. In early 1997 I had not yet read a word of Bruno Latour, and had only a loose familiarity with the major books of Alfred North Whitehead and Xavier Zubíri; over the following year these three authors would all play major roles in ending my career as a convinced if unorthodox Heideggerian. Until December of that year I was not even fully committed to realism, an essential part of my position ever since.

By 2009, things were rather different. By then I had published four books and traveled to fifty-seven countries. I was a veteran professor and newly minted administrator at the American University in Cairo, Egypt. Perhaps most importantly, I was associated in the public eye with a small group of like-minded philosophers called the Speculative Realists, none of them remotely known to me in 1997. These days, Speculative Realism is a well-known phrase with especial appeal to the younger generation in continental philosophy. The essays and lectures found here tell my own part of the story as a champion of the "object-oriented" wing of the movement. Rather than a unified school, Speculative Realism has always been a loose umbrella term for four markedly different positions: my own object-oriented philosophy, Ray Brassier's eliminative nihilism, Iain Hamilton Grant's cyber-vitalism, and Quentin Meillassoux's speculative materialism. In some respects these positions are incompatible, but as their collective name indicates, all combine a realist element with a speculative one. By "realist" I mean that these philosophies all reject the central teaching of Kant's Copernican Revolution, which turns philosophy into a meditation on human finitude and forbids it from discussing reality in itself. By "speculative" I mean that none of them merely defend a dull commonsense realism of genuine trees and billiard balls existing outside the mind, but a darker form of "weird realism" bearing little resemblance to the presuppositions of everyday life.

While numerous friends and well-wishers helped me to evolve from an unknown graduate student into a visible philosophical author, two in particular should be mentioned, since each is the subject of a lecture contained in this volume. From as early as 1990 it was Alphonso Lingis who kept me on the right path by example and encouragement. His strikingly realist version of phenomenology along with his stirring prose, offbeat lifestyle, and our shared background as small-town Midwestern Americans who wanted to see the world, were a great inspiration during my mostly frustrating years of graduate study. From 1999 onward I benefitted from personal contact with another genuine philosopher, Bruno Latour, whose irreverent wit and focus on specific entities were the perfect medicine for my post-Heideggerian hangover. Above all, Latour's unmatched intellectual versatility pointed the way to new communication with neighboring disciplines. Indeed, much of my reading audience is borrowed from his own, and I have adapted to this audience in ways that feel healthy.

For each chapter I have written a brief introductory paragraph explaining the circumstances under which the piece was written. Some of them were professional failures, rejected by conferences or unappreciated by those who heard them. Others were striking successes. The point of these notes is not to dramatize my own story, but to reassure young readers about their own. My road to the present was riddled with obstacles: often self-created, but sometimes acts of sabotage by tyrants. Yet the pleasure of writing the essays and giving the lectures was a great consolation over the years, and I hope they have a warm and inviting tone for those who read them now.

1. Phenomenology and the Theory of Equipment (1997)

This piece was a conference paper submitted in February 1997 to the Society for Phenomenology and Existential Philosophy (SPEP). The submission was rejected. Since 1991-92 I had placed the tool-analysis at the center of my interpretation of Heidegger, though at the time of writing this piece I was not yet a philosophical "realist" as was the case from December 1997 onward. Also missing from this essay is my later preoccupation with the role of das Geviert *or "the fourfold" in Heidegger, though this concern was already paramount from as early as 1994 when his "Einblick in das was ist"[1] was finally published in full. A few key phrases from the following paper later found their way into my first book,* Tool-Being *(2002).[2]*

Few passages in Heidegger's writings have attained as much notoriety as the analysis of equipment in *Being and Time*. It is impossible to find a summary of this work that does not make frequent reference to the vivid description of the tool and its malfunction. Still, the theme of equipment has rarely been pursued as a worthy problem in its own right. On one front, the concept of the tool is regarded as an early version of a later, full-blown meditation on the essence of technology. Elsewhere, one speaks of Heidegger's "pragmatist" period; from there, a debate erupts as to whether or not this pragmatism has anything to do with the philosopher's later concerns. A third camp, which includes many of the most reliable commentators, regards the tool-analysis as possessing a largely historical function, as a settling of accounts with the ancient poiesis/praxis distinction. But in each of these cases the real action is assumed to lie elsewhere, in one of the more remote and complicated themes of Heidegger studies. The current paper will argue against this tendency. First, we will show that Heidegger's account of tools is applicable not just to widely-recognized examples of handyman's tools (hammers, drills), but to every possible entity. Second, we will suggest that *all* of the more widely admired Heideggerian themes are derivatives of the philosopher's simple analysis of utensils. Finally, we will make a tentative suggestion concerning the development of a concrete theory of equipment.

The analysis of equipment is familiar enough that any paraphrase quickly becomes tedious. Our primary mode of encounter with entities, Heidegger shows, is not that of running across entities indifferently present-at-hand for perception. When the tool is most a tool, it recedes into a reliable background of subterranean machinery. Equipment is invisible. Furthermore, tools do not occur in isolation. Their meaning is determined by their definitive role in a referential contexture, their distinct position in this reality. The same hammer can be magnificent against soft wood, useless against metallic surfaces, and a lethal horror to many insects. In this way, the tool is what it is only with respect to the system it inhabits; there is no such thing as "an" equipment. Equipment is total, or contextural. What this tells us is that equipment, insofar as it is currently in use, is never something merely present-at-hand. Some part of the physical tool may stay in view, but its action necessarily withdraws into a totality that cannot become visible *in principle*. The tool is the execution of a reality or effect that necessarily retreats behind the presence of any surface. But this reality is not merely negative, as though self-concealment were its most striking feature. The tool is a force that exists rather than not existing, a reality that has emerged into the world and set up shop. Of course in the strict sense we should speak here not of tools, but rather of a single unitary world in action. For at this point we are not yet in position to regard an individual piece of gear as anything but illusory, as an ontic nullity with respect to its underground reality.

Let these remarks suffice to remind us of the basic features of Heidegger's innovative research concerning equipment. At the same time, we should not fail to notice that the scope of his analysis soon expands far beyond the limited number of objects normally classified as tools. Heidegger does not mean to talk about spoons and forks, as he will later point out on another occasion. Rather, every conceiveable entity is nothing less than an item of equipment. No being can be reduced to its presence-at-hand. The most useless flake of stone does not escape the system of tools; the tiniest grain of sand is what it is, surging into existence and throwing its weight around. No matter how negligible these entities are, they are not without their significance, even if for most humans it is the feeble significance of "triviality". Beneath its indifferent surface every entity occupies a highly determinate position in the system of significance that forms the world. In short, the analysis of tools is concerned only incidentally with the human *use* of tools. Its real subject matter is the stance of entities themselves in the midst of reality. The bridge is not a bridge due to the fact that Dasein uses it; the reverse is the case. A tool isn't "used"; it "is".

It will be objected that we have already missed the central significance of Dasein in this analysis. It will be claimed that Dasein is the key, since everyone knows that *Being and Time* is compromised by a transcendental standpoint in which human being is always taken as the final standard of reference. But there is a rarely noticed ambiguity in Heidegger's use of the term "Dasein". Admittedly, the human being is not the same kind of entity as a stone. Human beings partly transcend the entities that surround them, while the rock is merely the oblivious punching bag of the forces that mass against it. In more familiar terms, Dasein is gifted with an "understanding of being". Ignoring for now the difficult problem posed by animals, the human being seems to be a unique entity in precisely this way. But there is another trait of Dasein, one that is mentioned in an even earlier passage: the fact that Dasein's essence lies in its existence. Never meant to be sized up as a "rational animal" or as the "fusion of body and soul", Dasein can only be understood in the very act of its existence. Any claim to define Dasein via some representation or eidos or by way of any external properties is incapable of living up to the task. But this irreducibility of Dasein to a representation is also shared by hammers, and even by sand and rocks. We have already seen that *none* of these entities can be understood as if they were simply *vorhanden*. Readiness-to-hand does not mean "usable by people", but rather "sheer performance of an effect". Thus, Dasein in the second sense is *the absolute equivalent of the tool*, however counterintuitive this might seem. The distinctiveness of human Dasein has to be sought elsewhere. In addition, the fact that no entity whatsoever can be reduced to presence-at-hand means that Heidegger's famous distinction between categories and existentiales is misleading. Indeed, it is the great merit of his analysis of equipment to have exploded any possible notion of present-at-hand categories. Strictly speaking, categories are an illusion.

We return momentarily from the question of Dasein to the theme of tools in general. A brief while ago we recalled both the invisibility and the totality of the tool, traits that emerged from Heidegger's own account of equipment. These features described the character of entities in themselves, their primary mode of being, and not just the way in which people encounter them. If entities were invisible and total in the strict sense, we obviously would not encounter individual beings at all. All objects would fade away into an instantaneous global action, a system without organs. But experience shows that we do encounter singular entities; life is absorbed in nothing but such specific beings: sun, melons, puppets. How does Heidegger account for this duality? The most famous place is in his discusion of the "broken tool". The working piece of equipment is unobtrusive; in contrast, the malfunctioning instrument thrusts itself rudely into view. In this new "broken" situation, we gain a view of what was previously taken for granted. Equipment is no longer a silent laborer; it has surfaced as a visible power. It is a tool which has suddenly reversed into tool "as" tool. The visible world is the world of the "as", a tangible and volatile surface derived from a more primary dimension of being.

The realm of the broken tool is the realm of the "as". But just as the term "equipment" could not be limited to tools in the narrow sense, so the broken tool quickly reaches beyond the strict boundaries suggested by its name. Even a rough examination will show that Heidegger begins to define virtually everything in the same way as his concept of the broken tool. Space, for example, comes to be defined as nothing other than the freeing of entities from the anonymous referential contexture, in such a way that they take on a specific unique location of their own; this leaves us with no understanding of the difference between such heterogenous realms as spatial locations and broken hammers. The same holds true for the analysis of theory. Theory is shown to be the derivative of a work-world that is already experienced in advance; in this way theory, space, and broken tool have fused together into an indistinguishable brotherhood. Additional and related concepts could easily be listed here. But these three themes are enough to suggest that the idea of the reversal between equipment and the "as" dominates a substantial portion of Heidegger's work. Indeed, the justly praised Lecture Course of 1929/30[3] is misread when one accepts at face value Heidegger's apparent claim that he is offering us a course on life-philosophy. An unbiased reading of the text will show that 1929/30 is not a course on life at all, but only an investigation of the "as". From out of all the traditionally recognized characteristics of life (locomotion, nutrition, reproduction) Heidegger focuses only on the faculty of perception. And he does this in such a way that all of his attempted distinctions between what is human and what pertains to the animal rest upon a (finally unconvincing) gradation in the kind of "as" accessible to each species. With this remark we return to the first and most familiar sense of Dasein: Dasein as the being that has an understanding of being. It should now be clear that the perception of a broken hammer is an understanding of hammer "as" hammer; likewise, Dasein's understanding of being is an understanding of being "as" being. But in several instances we have seen that something like the "as" can only emerge from out of a prior contexture of equipment. Thus, the supposedly central problem of Dasein and its understanding is thoroughly dependent on a clearer solution of what occurs in the reversal between tool and broken tool, or tool and space. In short, the human Dasein is not a privileged entity by any means. The special features of this Dasein can only be understood in view of the analysis of simple equipment.

We repeat: Heidegger's central contribution to philosophy lies in his ruthless critique of presence-at-hand. And this critique is already worked out in sufficient form in his analysis of equipment. The introduction of the term "Dasein" makes sense only as an attempt to undercut any present-at-hand determination of the essence of man; Heidegger flatly tells us that this is the goal of introducing the term. Further, the question of being is rendered intelligible only as a challenge to the presence-at-hand of any object whatever. It may be wondered whether any of Heidegger's most widely appreciated terminology (time, *Ereignis*) ever drifts out of the orbit of the war against *Vorhandenheit*. On the whole, too much honor is granted to the withdrawn status of "being" (and its successors), too much effort wasted in an attempt to penetrate back beyond all known horizons into some even deeper unthematized site, where ultimately even being itself is supposed to be lodged. In fact the key to Heidegger's being is not its absolute concealment, but its absolute reality, its definitive action. We have argued elsewhere that despite all appearances to the contrary, the question of the meaning of being is answered very rapidly in *Being and Time*: the meaning of being is tools. This formulation can only sound dubious, even laughable, as long as we cling to our prejudices about the sense of the words "tool" and "being" in the text. But an ubiased reading of the text will show that both concepts serve only to undercut the age-old regime of presence-at-hand. Just as being reverses into manifold beings, so the unitary empire of equipment swings about into individual tool-pieces. Whether we like it or not, the two terms refer to precisely the same reality. Being is tool-being.

This will obviously be a difficult point for most readers to accept, but the constraints of time demand that we move on without more detailed argument. But in passing, we can cite further anecdotal evidence for the thesis that Heidegger's work is dominated wire-to-wire by a repetitive attack upon all that is *vorhanden*. Namely, we could call attention to the fact that the most consistent rhetorical appeal throughout Heidegger's career is not to the *Sein* that is eventually abandoned, nor to the *Ereignis* that disappears and reappears in his works. Rather, it is the spirit of the word *bloß*, meaning "mere" or "merely". Choose nearly any text you please from any period in Heidegger's career, and you will find him continuing to take gratuitous stabs at his constant enemy: the continual threat of relapse into understanding concepts in a present-at-hand sense. *Being and Time* warns us that a system of things is not a mere sum of *realia* that serve to fill up a room. (It would be entertaining to write a paper arguing that they *are* such a mere sum of *realia*.) Later, the lectures on Hölderlin's *Der Ister* insist that the famous *polla ta deina* of the Antigone chorus does not refer to a mere pile of uncanny present-at-hand entities. Even more amusingly, the *Phenomenology of Religious Life* lecture course of 1921 points out that "the appearance of the Antichrist is no mere transient happening".[4] If these examples are not yet enough to prove the existence of Heidegger's "one thought", they at least demonstrate that he was limited to one great joke.

It is on this note that we pause to consider the fascinating critique of Husserl presented in 1925 in *History of the Concept of Time*. The interesting thing here is not whether Husserl is outdone by his student. The critique actually acts with less potency against Husserl than against certain readings of Heidegger, insofar as these readings do not realize the astonishing concreteness of the question of being as presented in 1925. With his fruitful interpretation of the phenomenological method, Heidegger verges on rereading Husserl as a forerunner in the onslaught against all that is *vorhanden* (a crucial historical claim, especially in light of his comparison of Husserl's phenomenology with Hegel's *Science of Logic*). By interpreting the apriori as a title for being rather than a structure related to the inutiting subject above all else, Heidegger already reads Husserl's "phenomenon" as an *event* rather than a perception, as a real being both concealed and mirrored by its successive adumbrations. Nonetheless, he regards the phenomenon as still in bondage to the primacy of representation. "The being of the phenomenon is never raised as a question." This can only mean that in spite of everything, Husserl's phenomenon is still present-at-hand.

Instead of this, the alternative is that beings are realities, actual entities (the latter term is borrowed from Whitehead). The phenomena, the things themselves, are in the act of being. There is not only a concealment of the being of the things, but a real relation between this being and the visible surface of the thing. This shadowy relation ought to be reflected upon in greater detail. We have seen briefly how Heidegger's thought tends to mobilize itself around the opposition between tool and broken tool. The reality that materializes from the strife between them is composed of all manner of haloes, auras, and emergent subterranean currents. But we cannot begin to classify these divergent realities, nor even offer a rough dstinction between broken tools, theory, and space, so long as we do no more than defer to Heidegger's findings on the genesis of exteriority from depth.

The Grail Quest for "the possibility of possibility" is far down the wrong road, as is the assumption that the regressive movement back toward *Ereignis* would be hopelessly tainted by any philosophical contact with specific entities. What is now needed is an inverted strategy, in the name of a fresh and concrete research into the secret contours of objects: a renewed occupation with the things themselves. Moreover, this proposal is not hypothetical. We already have in our possession the first efforts in this direction in such essays by Heidegger as "Das Ding", "Bauen Wohnen Denken", and certain passages of the writings on language, all of them witnessing his frantic attempt to retrieve a reflection on things: jugs, cups, shoes... A handful of important but manageable paradoxes and discoveries arise when we examine in this way the relation between a being and its being. But here we have only had the time to set the table for a further analysis of equipment, in the broadest sense of the term.

2. Alphonso Lingis on the Imperatives in Things (1997)

In October 1997 Alphonso Lingis visited the Department of Philosophy at DePaul University in Chicago, where I was then a doctoral student. Lingis had been my advisor as I earned a Master's Degree in Philosophy at Penn State during 1990-91. On 11 October a roundtable discussion was held, with several DePaul faculty members and graduate students presenting short papers in response to his work. The following was my contribution to that event, from which I was initially excluded by a powerful enemy on the faculty. In conceptual terms, this paper gives an early hint of the full-blown realism that first emerged two months later. While Lingis had argued that inanimate objects have an ethical force over us no less than humans do, I extended this claim to say that objects encounter imperatives in their own right, rather than merely providing humans with them.

It has often been noted that our encounter with other human beings displays a strange character. In the first instance the Other is a limited, specific object of the world. To this extent, his or her personality, body-type, and temperament can be considered as the net product of physical and chemical forces, easily reducible to a series of causal mechanisms. While the most extreme version of this materialism is generally held in low regard today, it can still be an interesting experiment to push this view as far as possible. Behind our most compelling thoughts, then, we imagine enzymal secretions giving rise to various brain-states. Behind our most flamboyant individual passions, we detect concealed hereditary cravings just now breaking into full bloom, or the first traces of a culture or family in a state of gradual decay. This can be done not only for our character traits, but for every last event that befalls us. The most devastating strokes of bad luck often result from trivial miscalculations; at the same time, a cynic might easily trace the rise of every friendship back to some concealed motive of utility. The ability to explain all human phenomena in terms of some indefinite set of underlying causes might be called the "depth perception" of the other.

But there is also what we might term the "surface sensitivity" toward human beings. In the words of Lingis: "the other is also *other*. To recognize the other as other is to sense the imperative weighing on his or her thought. It is to sense its imperative force...."[5] Not merely a product of a limitless chain of causal forces, the other is absorbed in some task, acts in accordance with the imperative summons lying before her mind, expends her energy in taking something seriously. The same is true for us ourselves, since even the most hardened egotist would never imagine that he alone is exempt from the conditions of physical reality, free from the sphere of natural laws that work upon all objects equally. The person is marked then by two separate currents; the person is an object reversing into an other, or an earthly force doubling up into a face. The imperative that calls me obliges me to understand the causes and grounds that unleash their energies within the world. Still, the other interrupts that movement, posits a law that commands me with an irreducible force. Amidst the realm of nature or thought, the other represents a sort of intruder.

To see the other as other, even to see myself as an autonomous agent, is to stand before an actual imperative, a sincere finality in the world that cannot be identical with the history that gave birth to it. We see the other as ordered not by biochemical laws and cultural codings, but by a task. Pierrot builds a wagon or juggles no matter whether Harlequin convinced him to do so, and no matter whether wine or fever makes him do it. The human actor is always locked in some stance toward the objects surrounding him; he is immersed in this sincerity, a behavioral candor that does not escape our notice, and that weighs on us with equal force. He is not, as Lingis puts it, a simple phosphorescent image streaking across our consciousness: "To recognize the other, Kant says, is to recognize the imperative for law that rules in the other. To recognize the other is to respect the other."[6] The human agent, whether self or other, has already doubled up into a surface. In this way the whole of the human realm is shown to consist of two basic principles: the other regarded as the nexus of conditioning forces and energies, and the other as *sincere* or as occupied with the world that surrounds her.

We can proceed further, since this sincerity of the world contains several distinct strands. We have already spoken of the upsurge of a face of the other from the subterranean causal layers that sustain him, the emergence into the daylight of the other's commanding imperative. This imperative is present in both the hero and the mediocrity, it is present whether she be constructing some kind of unusual device or enjoying the simple pleasure of eating fruits. The face is always a face, whatever the nobility or pettiness of what drives the other on through the years.

At the same time, the face is never just a brute fact. It casts shadows and haloes, compels us to confront it with this or that attitude, seducing us in this or that way: "The things are not only structures with closed contours that lend themselves to manipulation and whose consistency constrains us. They lure and threaten us, support and obstruct us, sustain and debilitate us, direct and calm us. They enrapture us with their sensuous substances and also with their luminous surfaces and their phosphorescent facades, their halos, their radiance and their resonances."[7] Luring and threatening us, laying claim to our energies in some particular way, the face is an *idol*. We began by seeing that the other reversed from a natural object, a sort of puppet under unceasing causal coercion, into a vulnerable actor in the world. But we now find that this sincerity is split in half as well. For on the one hand it is the absolute fact of our being seduced by the faces of the world; on the other, it is the specific realm of lures and threats posed by those faces, the full spectrum of blessings and curses unleashed into the world by this face that also takes the shape of an idol.

The other is both face and idol. But there is still another possibility, ever present along with the first two. The idol also becomes a *fetish*, a mask no longer drifting across the world like an independent power, but now used to manipulate or enslave. In the author's example:

> The professor who enters the classroom the first day has been preceded by the legend or myth of himself which the students now see materializing before their eyes. They adjust practically to the level of his voice and to the arena of his movements; he knows they are looking at the personage and fits his person into it as he enters the room. He will use this professorial mask to intimidate them.... When in the classroom he slouches over his papers and stifles a yawn, he is not simply shrinking back into a bare anatomy moved by fatigue, he is agitating his masks disdainfully or ironically.[8]

And again, "A fetish is used to obtain something one needs or wants; it is put forth in the service of one's fears or one's cupidity. The idol is noble; the fetish is servile."[9]

The imperative face, then, is by the same stroke both idol and fetish, and this is true in all instances. The pedant in the example just cited can modulate or oscillate his own self-generated caricature as much as he pleases, extending his personal dominance to a formidable degree. But even behind this jaded mask, the idol of a human face transmits its law through the air and commands a genuine response from us. Likewise, even the idolized face of a saint or a hero does not escape the inevitable fetishization of itself; human nature is too duplicitous for this. If seduction is an event, it is also always to some degree a tool used to fascinate, conquer, or even pillage the other. For this reason, the phenomena entitled "idol" and "fetish" are not so much distinct kinds of masks as they are inverse dimensions of a single inescapable fate: the fate of the image in its power over reality.

So far we have been discussing several distinct aspects of the imperative face of the other. To repeat, this imperative arises by way of a reversal in which the other as an object subjected to a crushing network of earthly laws and determinations reverses into the other as an autonomous commander, by virtue of the task he confronts us with. This is the point at which Lingis takes a step that never occurs even to Levinas: the structure of the imperative, it is claimed, lies even in the things themselves. As Lingis puts it, the corporeal element *of objects* doubles into an interior motor schema and an outward aspect, a duplication that no longer belongs to the human being alone: "When I look at the sequoias I do not focus on them by circumscribing their outlines; the width of their towering trunks and the shape of their sparse leaves drifting in the fog appear as the surfacing into visibility of an inner channel of upward thrust."[10] If this description is to be believed (and we believe it wholeheartedly) then even the sequoia, that mass of semi-aware organic material, presents a face to those who encounter it.

To speak of an "inner channel of upward thrust" in the tree itself is not a metaphor, or at least not primarily a metaphor. For what we see before us in the forest is not a large patch of brown color, nor even the settled datum of a tree-object onto which we could graft personifying tendencies. Instead, amidst the elemental chaos of the forest and its iridescent gloom and its infernal insect chants, we encounter something like a tree-effect. Amidst the primitive confusion of the terrestrial landscape, we run across something with the "style" of a tree. It doesn't have that apple look, that corncob feel, or that soybean air about it; rather, we sense that familiar sequoia thickness and grandeur. In this way the sequoia itself becomes idolized; the tree doubles up into an idol. And like any idol, it cannot protect itself from the role of a fetish. We can see this more easily in the author's own example of a pen, which he insists we do not encounter as a black cylindrical object, but rather as "the condensation of a somber power." This idol-worship of the pen as an ominous force gives way just as quickly to its simple appropriation for everyday tasks, picked up and used in a facile way by those no longer attuned to its "inner channel of horizontal thrust".

It is in this connection that the reader of these essays on the imperative encounters a remarkably fresh approach to the problem of technology. Historians of the tool have long noted that equipment externalizes human organs. The hammer prolongs the length and power of the human forearm, the telescope one-ups the eyeball, while internal combustion vehicles render obsolete the long-distance function of the legs. Given what has just been said about idol and fetish, we could say that all of these devices somehow de-fetishize the object, displace its usefulness and manipulability onto some external point, leaving behind the original object as a useless but gorgeous flower, as an orchid: "Orchids are plants with atrophied trunks and limbs, parasitically clinging to the rising trunks that shut out the sun, flowering their huge showy sex organs, awaiting the bees for their orgasmic unions."[11]

For this reason, perhaps far from stripping objects down into calculable reservoirs of fuel, the progress of technology is leading us toward a completely de-fetishized world, a landscape of imperative simulacra, a planet populated with orchid-like residues, phantom objects devoid of any serviceability. Lingis imagines the final stage of this process in a passage of ominous beauty: "Can we imagine at some future date the faculty of memory, reason, and decision disconnecting from the computers which it now serves, ceasing to be but an organ-for-apprehending, and, swollen with its own wonders, becoming an organ-to-be-apprehended, an orchid rising from the visceral and cerebral depths of the cybernetic forest with its own power, rising into the sun?"[12] For us at least, much of the appeal of this unique passage lies in the fact that it reads like anything but a warning.

The object is an imperative, radiating over us like a black sun, holding us in its orbit, demanding our attention, insisting that we reorganize our lives along its shifting axes. The object is a force, and thus our valuation of it is a gift of force, and nothing like a recognition at all. This fact leads the reader toward a series of remarks on language. The phrase "how beautiful you are!"[13] does not communicate information, but bows to your beauty or at least pretends to bow, expressing either your own seductive force or my own deceit. These evaluative terms also become especially clear, as the author indicates, in the speech of children: "bad fire", "dangerous street".[14] To respond to these objects populating the earth, and to the elemental medium that supports them, is to enter into the seductive chant of insects, the realm of solar expenditure and vegetative sexualities: "Life's blessing extends over a universe of riddles and dreadful accidents."

The servile are those who face others with their faces closed off from the world, who substitute for the vulnerability of their surface the indomitable power of a fetish. But "the idol glows with its own light".[15] That is to say, "the face refracts a double of itself, made of warmth and light, which speaks, not messages addressed to other orders, but vitalizing and ennobling.... We expose our carnal substance to the grandeur of the oceans and the celestial terror of electrical storms.... mantras with which an idol crystallizes."

We would like to end this summary with a question. We have seen that the other is at work, devoted to her task, and that this task commands us. Our question is whether this command really arises only within the narrow confines of human representation. The upward thrust of the sequoia commanded me to see it as an object, as a durable "sequoia style" amidst the scrambled hysteria of contradictory forest objects. But is it just that reality commands me to see this tree for what it is? Or does this giant tree itself, cutting across the ether, turning toward the sun, sucking juice from the soil, not already live in the domain of the imperative? Given the vast scope of this new interpretation of the imperative, it would be hard to deny this structure to wolves and dolphins, to the zebras racing across the savanna and the ravens playing pranks with clotheslines. Even the more widely despised organisms, the ones we all join in destroying (moths, beetles, microbes) must then be governed by an imperative as well.

And ultimately, this must be true even of inanimate matter itself: would it be necessary to reinterpret causality itself as a form of the imperative in things? A possible key to answering this question can be found in other passages from Lingis's *Foreign Bodies*, with which we will bring this summary to a close. The first runs as follows: "The things have to not exhibit all their sides and qualities, have to compress them behind the faces they turn to us, have to tilt back their sides in depth and not occupy all the field with their relative bigness, because they have to coexist in a field with one another and that field has to coexist with the fields of the other possible things."[16] Making room for one another in this way, objects contest each other, seduce each other, empower or annihilate each other. Commanding one another by way of the reality of their forces, the objects exist as imperatives. Like fish hunting food or dogs playing with balls, it is possible that gravel and tar, cloth and magnesium wage war against one another, compress one another into submission, command *respect* from one another.

The second passage runs as follows: "...as [the body] rows across waters it becomes for itself something seen by the lake and the distant shore; as it grapples with the rocks it takes on mass and weight.... But in letting loose its hold on things, letting its gaze get caught up in the monocular images, reflections, refractions, will-o'-the-wisps, our body dematerializes itself and metamorphoses into the drifting shape of a Chinese lantern among them."[17]A lantern among Aztec, eagle, sphinx, cobra, quetzal bird.

3. The Theory of Objects in Heidegger and Whitehead (1997)

This lecture was given at DePaul University on Halloween Night, 1997 to an audience containing many DePaul graduate students and faculty members Bill Martin and Angelica Nuzzo. Though I had made intermittent attempts to read Whitehead from as early as 1986, it was only during the summer of 1997 that Whitehead (and the great Spanish Basque philosopher, Xavier Zubíri) began to push me away from a largely Heideggerian standpoint. The following lecture was the first attempt to reorient my work on Heidegger under the influence of Whitehead's de-humanized ontology. The Heidegger section ends with another early hint of my quickly evolving view (inspired by Whitehead himself) that inanimate interactions display the same basic "as-structure" as human cognition. The interpretation of Whitehead offered in the second half has some unorthodox features, such as downplaying the term "societies" and treating all entities as "actual entities". But I would still be willing to defend this interpretation today.

The following lecture aims to provide a rapid but lively summary of the ontological views of Martin Heidegger and Alfred North Whitehead. It is possible that the combined work of these thinkers represents the highest point attained by first philosophy in the twentieth century. But while each of them is backed by literally thousands of admirers, these followers remain so factionalized, so mutually invisible, that it is rare to hear their two heroes praised with the same voice. All the same, it is not difficult to show that Heidegger and Whitehead are united in having pioneered a new *theory of objects* in philosophy, one that has not received adequate development from either camp. This claim does not imply any ultimate agreement between them on philosophical issues, any more than a shark and a squid agree by the mere fact of living in the same bay. But whatever the similarities

22

or differences between these two key figures, it will be necessary to approach them by way of two distinct strategies; in each case there is a unique difficulty.

The writings of Whitehead openly describe the world as a theater populated by countless objects: by electrons, x-rays, rocks, flowers, icicles, comets, and animals, as well as by musicians, scientists, copper mines, monasteries, and bombs. These stock characters scattered across the planet cannot help but affect each other: they enjoy or fear, block or destroy one another. Some entities endure for millenia. Others decay quickly through the damage of radiation and collision, or through violent inner turmoil. Today's lecture will largely defend this view of reality: that of the world as a system of duelling, seducing, turbulent objects, a standpoint that can be ascribed to Whitehead in a self-evident way. But insofar as Whitehead's great systematic work *Process and Reality* is probably unfamiliar to most listeners tonight, half of the present remarks will be occupied with clarifying his major terminology.

With Heidegger the problem is quite the opposite: his basic concepts are widely familiar to most advocates of continental philosophy, to such an extent that any simple overview of terms might be regarded by this audience as tedious. For this reason, the task with respect to Heidegger is different; namely, it has to be shown that the term "theory of objects" can be applied to Heidegger's thought at all. In his works we seem to encounter only passing references to hammers, jugs, and bridges, while the real drama apparently occurs elsewhere: within the sphere of historical human Dasein and its cryptic relation to being. Here I will argue exactly the contrary point, maintaining that Heidegger's insights force nothing less than a theory of objects upon us, that the supposedly privileged questioning human is only an interesting case of the crippling strife found even amidst soulless drops of water and dazed wild plants; furthermore, that far from requiring a detailed textual argument, this can already be made intuitively clear from the opening pages of *Being and Time* alone.

In this way, the first half of the lecture will offer a compact and unorthodox reading of Heidegger; the second, a less daring summary of Whitehead's basic intellectual position. The long-range goal of what is expressed here today is to help make room in present-day continental thought for a more audacious brand of speculative philosophy than is currently allowed.

Part I: Heidegger

If we ignore the various student theses collected in Volume 1 of the *Gesamtausgabe*, then *Being and Time* is not only Heidegger's greatest book, but his *first* book as well. If we ignore further the Introduction to this work (which was actually written after the rest), as well as the twenty-some pages on methodology that follow, we find that Heidegger's first public philosophical statement is his famous *analysis of tools*. While this fact is not of overwhelming importance in its own right, it is also no accident. In fact, it can be shown that every insight of Heidegger's philosophical career makes sense only in light of the description of equipment.

The analysis of the hammer elaborates neither a "pragmatism" nor a "priority of practical reason". In fact, the scenario of the tool in *Being and Time* has nothing to do with the human use of tools, and everything to do with the tools themselves. Walking across a bridge, I am adrift in a world of equipment: the girders and pylons that support me, the durable power of concrete beneath my feet, the dense unyielding grain of the topsoil in which the bridge is rooted. What looks at first like the simple and trivial act of walking is actually embedded in the most intricate web of tool-pieces, tiny implanted devices watching over our activity, sustaining or resisting our efforts like transparent ghosts or angels. Each of these objects executes a specific effect amidst reality. Bolts and trestles are not neutral facts, but exert a definitive power in the cosmos on the basis of their particular thickness and tensile strength. Forever contending with one another, these tool-beings throw their weight around in the world, each of them ensconced in some small niche of reality.

Seen in this way, the tool has two major characteristics. The first is its invisibility. Bridge-panels and rivets do their work unnoticed, slipping away into an unnoticed backdrop while their labors are silently relied upon. Note that this is true even of equipment born in the pre-human past: air pressure condensing near our skin, or the gravity draining every object toward the cores of planets and suns. The important point is not so much that these tool-elements are *manipulated* by us; rather, they form a total cosmic infrastructure of artificial and natural and perhaps supernatural forces, powers by which our every last action is besieged. In short, the tool isn't "used"; it *is*. The work of being that makes up the tool's reality forever recedes from view. This is its first trait. The second is its *totality*. No tool operates in a vacuum; ontology allows for no action at a distance. The most irrelevant nail or square of asphalt is already shipwrecked in an environment of cement, bridge-cable, vehicles, tremors, and random vibrations. Furthermore, the bridge has a completely different reality for every entity it encounters: it is utterly distinct for the seagull, the idle walker, and those who may be driving across it toward a game or a funeral. The impact of all equipment, the reality of tool-beings, is entirely dependent on its shifting position in various systems of reality.

We can see that in the first instance, the tool recedes from every possible view. What Heidegger calls the ready-to-hand is said to remain invisible except for certain special cases, the most famous case of this kind being the "broken tool". In most instances, a driver's attention is focused on the car as an integral unit, on its various uses, benefits, and drawbacks; only the damage or utter malfunction of an engine or fuel-line reminds us that the car is made of vulnerable, finite pieces. When the tool breaks, Heidegger says, we lose our simple reliance on the tool and become aware of it "as" the tool that it is. At this point an important oversight often occurs. There is a common but misguided tendency to read Heidegger's broken tool as a kind of empirical anecdote ("Have you ever noticed that when we're using something, we usually don't pay attention to it?"). In fact, something far more radical is at stake. No matter how badly the tool breaks, now matter how deeply we dissect or analyze it, whatever emerges will *never* be the tool in its being, in the silent and faceless action through which it joins in the universe of forces. More simply put: there is an absolute gulf between Heidegger's readiness-to-hand and presence-at-hand. No real passage between them is possible, since the tool as a brutal subterranean energy and as a shining tangible surface are utterly incommensurable. Stated differently, the as-structure is incapable of variation or improvement. No matter how many facets of the engine we eventually unveil or catalog for ourselves, we cannot possibly draw any closer to the tool in its being than we already were.

We can also mention a second, equally common mistake made by readers of Heidegger. This is the assumption that the terms "ready-to-hand" and "present-at-hand" are meant to classify two different types of objects: the first composed of drills, chisels, or saws, the second made up of natural entities such as trees, clouds, and "useless" chunks of dirt. On one side, it is thought, handy shovels and trains; on the other side, non-human forests, caverns, and lagoons. This separation can easily be shown to be incorrect. In the first place, even officially sanctioned tools such as hammers are frequently found in present-at-hand form: as when they sit idly by, not involved in any current activity. At the same time, it should be clear that *every* entity is ready-to-hand: not in the derivative sense of "means to an end", but in the primary sense of "in the act of being", of unleashing itself upon the environment. Far from describing two kinds of entities, Heidegger's *vorhanden* and *zuhanden* describe a universal dualism found in all entities, a reversal that occurs in human beings and dogs every bit as much as in inanimate matter. Since this reversal or *Umschlag* is meant as a translation of Aristotle's *metabole*, all ontology is metontology, a valuable term that Heidegger himself abandons too quickly. All of reality, he shows, lies in a state of "metabolism" between the unchecked fury of tool-beings and the alluring facades through which alone we encounter them.

Then equipment is global; beings are tool-beings. Entities are torn between the performance of their irreducibly veiled activity and the warmth of their sparkling contours. This means that Heidegger's discussion of tools is not just a local bulletin about the breakdown of hammers; instead, whether intentionally or not, philosophy itself has been utterly redefined as the theme of tool and broken tool, the constant reversal of the concealed action of things into a sensible and explorable profile. It can also be shown that every attempt on Heidegger's part to escape this simple and repeated dualism soon collapses back into the scenario of the tool and its malfunction.

His account of theory, for example, does no more than show us that the as-structure emerges from a prior contexture of meaning; theory is not born in isolation, but exists by uncovering the unthematic meanings in which we are involved before theoretical comportment ever appears. But unfortunately this also turns out to be true even of the most apathetic pre-theoretical stupor or of states of stunned disorientation, despite Heidegger's efforts to give theory a higher rank. Even in these cases, Dasein is thrown into a world that is still somehow revealed to it in such and such a way.

The same is true of space as well; for Heidegger, spatiality too only frees objects from the universal system of meaning into distinct, concrete regions. But it should be noticed that this occurs even for non-spatial reality, as when a background mood of ecstasy or despair suddenly becomes clear in our minds. Thus, even the accounts of space and theory give us only further examples of the reversal between tool and tool "as" tool, and tell us nothing unique about theory or space themselves. The progress of *Being and Time* from the hammer-analysis onward is not an expansion: it is an implosion, a devouring of all possible specific problems by the unique question of the system of tools and its breakdown into recognizable parts. Since none of these terms (broken tool, theory, space) ever attain any real difference for Heidegger, we can use them as absolute synonyms: code words pointing back to a repeated primal duality he is unable to escape. For this reason, in addition to the "theory of tools and broken tools", we might also call Heidegger's thought a "philosophy of the *as*", or a "philosophy of tools and space".

Ultimately, the same fate befalls even his concept of "temporality", although this claim will be more controversial. To make our point, we can return to the earlier analysis of the bridge. We saw that the bridge did not exist simply as an obvious physical block; instead, its reality differed completely depending upon the specific hopes and fears of the observer. Heidegger's term for the relation of such an observer to that which is encountered is simply "projection". Whoever meets up with this bridge-thing draws it into a system of meaning defined by the terminal point of their actions; projection *is* Heidegger's "futuricity", and it is found in every situation. Equally, human Dasein projects possibilities only upon that which it already finds alongside itself; in other words, the tool-beings themselves are what is past. In spite of continued misleading efforts to place the structure of temporality outside of specific things, in spite of the continued tendency of most Heideggerians to treat specific objects with as much respect as smallpox, ecstatic temporality is nothing other than the ever-present duel between the occult receding action of the tool and the radiant profile that emerges into view according to the position in reality of the observer. The bridge-effect is past, timelessly past, but it appears as a different force to reckon with for seagulls, fishermen, street vendors, and commandoes.

But now comes a subtler and more controversial point: the analysis of the temporality of the bridge actually has nothing to do with time at all. As unbelievable as it may sound, Heidegger offers us no theory of time whatsoever. We can imagine that time is suddenly frozen in its tracks, with the universe petrified forever in its current stance. Heidegger cannot prevent this thought experiment. The idea that time cannot be reduced to individual cinematic frames is not to be found in his writings, as is sometimes wrongly assumed; this is actually the view of Bergson, and marks an insight that Heidegger simply never addresses. Note that even in our imaginary situation devoid of time, even with all hope of a real future gone forever, Heidegger's ecstatic analysis still works. Even here, every organism encountering the bridge encounters it in some specific way, confronts it with some particular projection, no matter whether tomorrow ever comes. As Levinas sees so clearly, what Heidegger gives us is not a theory of the flow of time, but an unprecedented systematic articulation of the instant. In other words, Heidegger's objection to regarding time as a sequence of now-points is not effective against the now-points, but only against the *sequence*; as long as the "now" is not taken as an obvious present-at-hand unit, the failing of traditional theories of time has already been avoided. In sum, there is nothing in the celebrated Heideggerian theory of time except yet another version of the strife between tool and broken tool or execution and surface: between the thing in its being and the so-called "temporal" projection that deploys that thing somewhere in our awareness. Therefore, another synonym for what we have called Heidegger's philosophy of tools and broken tools, or tools and space, would be a theory of *being and time*. And this is what is

this entity is said to be an understanding of its being. Dasein not only is itself, as even paper and dust are; more than this, Dasein somehow *grasps* the being of the beings it encounters. But the notion that this makes Dasein a kind of transcendental starting point for the question of being is clearly false, even when Heidegger seems to read himself in this way. Any grasping or seeing of which Dasein is capable does not occur in isolation. All such understanding must occur through the mediation of the as-structure: being is understood "as" such-and-such; rock and scissors are understood "as" what they are rather than as something else. But the "as" exists only in its emergence from the prior reality of the thing understood: in the theater of the tool and its breakdown, in the widest sense of these terms. Then the key to *Being and Time* is not the existential analytic of Dasein, which only collapses all possible moods and events into a single ambivalent point, but rather the first analysis of tool-beings.

It will now be useful to place additional weight on an important issue that has arisen several times already: the abuse of the as-structure. This structure of perception means that the tools themselves somehow become visible "as" what they are, like the broken hammer that unveils its previously hidden function. But we have said that whatever becomes visible in this way cannot possibly be the same as the tool in its effectiveness. There is nothing that could ever make the dark underground of the object's secret life congruent with the perceptible hammer-apparition that now hovers before our eyes. These are incommensurable realities, different worlds. In more familiar terms, the hammer-effect can never come to presence. But not only is it impossible for the hammer itself to come to view; we also cannot appeal to the hammer itself as a regulative telos, as an ideal limit case at which our successive explorations of the hammer would at least *aim*. Even a lazy view of the bridge grasps this bridge to some extent "as" what it is, rather than simply depending upon it; we get no closer to the bridge itself even if we study it rigorously under the best-planned test conditions.

We can take an example from elsewhere in Heidegger's writings: the case of Angst, in which Dasein is said to be held out into the nothing. The problem is that Heidegger goes on to say that Dasein is *always* held out into the nothing, so that when apparently absent Angst is really only "asleep", as he puts it. But he cannot have it both ways. He cannot say that the nothing pervades reality everywhere and at all times, and also salute Angst as the experience of nothingness *par excellence*. For even Angst has no privileged relation to the nothing "as" nothing; opacity hinders the as-structure here as much as anywhere else. This is one possible and necessary way of turning the results of Derrida's *Speech and Phenomena* against Heidegger's self-understanding. In any case, the misuse of the "as" as an assymptotic approach to the things themselves is rendered completely invalid.

Heidegger often draws a distinction between *gründen* and *stiften*, the "grounding" accomplished by the thinker and the "instituting" brought about the poet. The work of grounding should in principle be able to unearth the dark background conditions of any event, bringing them into explicit view. We have now seen that this cannot be done, that the background effect of equipment can never become visible in the least, not even approximately. For the same reason, by Heidegger's own standards, grounding is *impossible*. For this reason, perhaps even more incredibly, truth cannot possibly be *aletheia*. Like the as-structure itself, the Janus-head of veiling and unveiling always sits still; no movement of unconcealment can ever bring us an inch closer to the tool itself in its executant reality. Whatever the champions of Heidegger's "turn" want to say, the phrase "being and truth" tells us no more about reality than the words "tool and broken tool" already told us.

If grounding is impossible, there remains only one alternative in Heidegger's system, whether for philosophy or poetry or anything else: *stiften, bilden, bauen;* instituting, forming, building. For the moment, this alternative remains completely vague, yet it is a promising option at least in negative terms. That which is "formed" or "built" for Heidegger is usually a symbol, whether it be a knot in a handkerchief or an image in the midst of a poem by Trakl. Language as a whole is often referred to by Heidegger as a formation of symbols or signs. But before following the contemporary habit and placing the full weight of philosophy on the theme of language, we should notice other uses of *bilden* in Heidegger. The organism *forms* its organ, which is hardly a symbol in the narrow sense of the term. And even in reference to the inanimate jug, Heidegger tells us that *es bildet sich eine Leere*: "an emptiness forms" in the midst of the jug.

For the moment, there is no need to discuss the positive features of this broader form of symbolizing. The important factor here is still a negative one. The symbol is not the mere evoking of a ground, stationary in its immovable dualism. Every formation of a sign is different, and concretely different: thus any object can only be understood as a kind of *bilden*, the instituting of an utterly concrete type of reality. A satellite unlocks powers that are unknown to landmines or medicines, and the book is a different medium from a sword or a carbon atom. Another way to put this is to say that objects are media, natural or artificial agents set loose into the world like wild animals: just as enchanting, and every bit as deadly.

Any object is a complex and irreducible event; like the moon, one face of the tool is darkened in the silence of its orbit, while another face illuminates and compels us with dazzling surface-effects. No object, however banal, is just the empty represen- tative of a standing reserve of calculable presence. However naive an object might seem, it still makes its incisions into being, exploding with power at a level always escaping our view. Heidegger's failure to zero in on this fact leads him to make several claims so easy to attack that it can seem like grandstanding to do so, and thus we must do it quickly. If we understand technology as the triumph of presence over the epochal withdrawal of being, we will have fallen back into precisely the inadequacies of the misemployed as-structure. In this case, no concrete difference between objects could possibly be regarded as anything but vulgar. It will seem like an unimportant step from the stone axe to the hydrogen bomb, or from cloned wheat seeds to millions of dead bodies. Furthermore, in terms of the history of philosophy, it will seem as if an entire roster of concepts (eidos, *actus*, monad...) were merely interchangeable epiphenomena of a growing forgetfulness of being, a regime of presence-at-hand whose transformations through the ages can only seem like an afterthought.

While Heidegger's much-admired destruction of the history of ontology does display an awesome sum of learning, it also contains few surprises for anyone familiar with the first three or four volumes' worth of it. Like so many other Heideggerian themes, the historical destruction is actually an implosion in which the entire history of philosophy has its feet held to the fire of presence-at-hand, Heidegger's single lifelong enemy. This is why, despite Heidegger's stature in the philosophy of the twentieth century, his obvious superior as a reader of historical texts is Deleuze. For it is Deleuze who defines philosophy (interestingly enough) as a "creation of concepts", and then correctly describes these concepts as independent forces traversing and apportioning reality, cybernetic devices as noble and clean as the tigers of Bengal.

We can now bring this summary of Heidegger to a close with one very important note. Criticizing the misuse of the as-structure as a measuring stick instead of just the unvarying reality that it is, we opposed to "grounding" (which is impossible) Heidegger's other concept of founding or building or instituting. But even this alternative remains locked within the stifling horizon of the ever-present duality between the tool and its breakdown. Not a single square inch of the cosmos has been spared from the dominance of this obsessive opposition.

Only by pushing Heidegger's as-structure to its point of absolute dominance do we gain a genuine thirst for that which escapes it. And such a thing does exist: a rarely noticed second axis that cuts across the familiar Heideggerian drama of concealed and revealed, tool and broken tool. This second principle is actually dominant in Heidegger's thought as early as 1919, but to avoid a distracting detour, we can summarize it out of context as follows. It turns out that there is not only a duality between the tool and its appearance; rather, appearance itself is also torn apart by two separate currents. As becomes especially clear in Angst, but as is always true, there is a difference between the specific content of any perception and the simple fact that we are delivered over to that perception at all, no matter what it is. An appearance is not only the emergence of a concealed tool into concrete form; it also commands our sincerity rather than being nothing, causes us to expend our vital energy in taking it seriously. As one underrated contemporary thinker might put it: the object is not only a simulation, but a seduction as well.[18] But an identical split occurs on the level of the invisible tools. Rock and paper in themselves are not merely the execution of an anonymous force; their reality has a certain character or *consistency*, in the sense that we can speak of the consistency of a liquid or a snow. And this is true quite apart from any perception of these objects. Already, it is easy enough to see that this second principle of division is a remote successor to the traditional gulf between existence and essence.

To repeat, there are *two* axes of reality for Heidegger. Part of the difficulty in seeing this stems from his indiscriminate use of the term "ontological difference" to refer to both. In any case, the result of having two first principles rather than one is that the typical Heideggerian schema of tool and broken too is suddenly complexified. Reality is split into quadrants: the thing becomes a fourfold. Even if this weren't the same as Heidegger's own inscrutable fourfold (although in fact it is), it would still deserve to be analyzed in its own right as an inescapable feature of the reality of equipment. A further possible thesis, which cannot be developed here, is that the relation of the quadrants within the object itself make up the original form of *stiften*, a counterposing of the axes of reality along and against one another. If the fourfold defines the thing as a sort of manifold atom, the "building" or "forming" of sign-objects as described by Heidegger must somehow split the atom, so as to make the creation of new realities possible. Thus, objects might be regarded as media that somehow manage to unlock the tension within the world's quadrants.

In finishing up these prolonged remarks on Heidegger, it should be asked if the fourfold exists only for human observers, or at least only for sentient organisms. After all, inanimate objects do not really seem to encounter other objects "as" what they are. But in actuality they do, as can be argued briefly enough. Imagine that a three-ounce weight and a one-ton weight are both dropped from the same height onto an empty house. The smaller weight encounters the house on some primitive level "as" a barrier, as an obstacle on its downward flight. The larger weight will hardly be resisted at all, and might pick up only a couple of scratches as it smashes the house to the ground; thus, it runs up against the house "as" a contemptible pseudo-barrier. All objects encounter all other objects "as" such and such: "as" destructible, impenetrable, formidable. This is not to say that the weight is conscious of the house; it is only to say that what we call "consciousness" must involve something much more than the as-structure, which is absolutely primitive. This means that consciousness too is something that builds and is built rather than something that only grounds or unveils. Conscious awareness must be viewed as a more advanced form of perceptive machinery, inexplicable by mere reference to the "as" and its dark twin, the tool.

As a smooth transition to Whitehead, we can introduce a new term for this relation of weights and rocks and windstorms to the house: *prehension*, as opposed to explicit apprehension. Rock prehends air; fire prehends paper; Dasein prehends shovel.

Part II: Whitehead

The primary realities for Whitehead are "actual entities," a term from which no type of object is excluded. God is an actual entity, as are people; hair and dirt are actual entities, and vague magnetic currents in distant space are actual entities as well. As such, all of them are instantaneous and definite forces, utterly determined by their stance in the universe with respect to all other objects. But actual entities are not substances; they are not the unchanging subjects of change. This rock now and this rock an instant from now are not the same actual entity; the later rock is at best a close successor of the historical rock that precedes it. To emphasize the fact that one actual entity does not undergo adventures in time and space, Whitehead often replaces the term "actual entity" with "actual occasion". In the strict sense there would have to be only one actual entity: the universe, in which all specific objects are locked into relation with one another.

This relation between actual entities is what Whitehead terms "prehension". All objects prehend all others, even if in most cases the intensity of this prehension is close to zero. The rock and the glass it smashes clearly prehend each other, as do all objects in any kind of immediate or semi-immediate connection. But equally so, the tiniest alteration in a remote corner of the universe alters, however slightly, the potentiality locked in this rock and this glass here on earth, transforms in some minute way their energy with respect to the world as a whole. Entities affect other entities. The ontological effect of a distant event on this rock-object here is only apparently an action at a distance. In metaphysical terms, there is no dstance; reality is a plenum, in which every slightest oscillation of a grain of sand redefines the structure of objects millions of light years away. This openness of entities to one another, this saturation of beings with windows, means that consciousness is only a special case of experience. All entities have mental as well as physical life. "The philosophy of organism abolishes the detached mind", he tells us, the phrase "philosophy of organism" being Whitehead's favorite name for himself. The sensationalism of Hume, Kant, and others is rejected, since sense-data are regarded as an arbitrary and narrow restriction of the field of experience, of objects relating to one another by way of prehension.

In all prehension, three factors can be found: the actual entity, the entity it prehends, and the "how" of this prehension. This "how" takes the shape of what Whitehead calls "eternal objects". Taken together, actual entities and eternal objects make up all that exists; everything else is said only to clarify the interaction between these two realities. An actual entity such as a star is the site of innumerable forces, the locus of an absolute effect mirrored in all other beings. But other entities do not encounter the star in quite this way. Rocks, comets, plants, and humans each "objectify" the star differently, encounter it in some specific and limited way that does not exhaust the full of its reality. The full content of an actual entity is irrelevant to the other entities, which limit it to a specific site in their experience, however minimal this may be. This occurs by means of the eternal objects, which Whitehead regards as the rough equivalent of the Platonic forms. Only one entity can have the same real essence, the same absolute actuality of being what it is. But many entities have the same *abstract* essence: many entities are green or noisy or bear the forces of physical causation within themselves. There is no permanent substance, but *forms* are permanent: hence the name "eternal objects", which simply expresses the identity of these ideas in the objectification of utterly different actual entities. The forms or ideas an object has of other objects show the specific way in which other things enter as ingredients into its own constitution.

As a system of forces, the world is a tightly compressed continuum. For Whitehead, this is the meaning of extension, which exists as the field of all potentiality for the universe as presently constituted. The actuality of an actual entity is at the same time its potentiality for being objectified in such-and-such a way by every other object that exists. But by objectifying its fellow objects, an entity transforms the continuous potentiality of the extenssive scheme into a set of atomic realities, trans-forming them from forces into objects. We saw that all entities prehend or experience one another; another way to say this is that they all "feel" one another. Then the eternal object, by which other realities are objectified, can be considered as a "lure" for feeling, as a way in which the concealed action of those realities is pressed into taking on a tangible, definite form. Whitehead calls this process "concrescence". To objectify something is to repeat its reality, but under the limited perspective that is necessary for it ever to be given at all.

In the case of human beings, there is obviously freedom involved in this process, since many different objectifications of the entities around us are possible. Life runs its course within the theater of these eternal objects. Whitehead claims that this is true even at the inanimate level, that there is always some minuscule leeway of freedom by which the object can bring other entities to givenness. Freedom thus becomes an ontological principle rather than just a specifically human or animal reality, a notion probably inspired by the quantum theory in which Whitehead was so deeply involved. The freedom of even the minutest particles of reality yields at least one important practical result: the so-called laws of nature are only abstractions from the drama of the actual entity in its free objectification of the cosmos. For this reason, the apparently invariable laws of gravitation and electromagnetic force can only be assumed to hold true for our own specific "cosmic epoch". There is a gradual evolution of matter and its types of prehensions just as there is a development of animal species. Somewhat cryptically, we are told that God alone rises beyond the traits of the current cosmic era.

This is where a somewhat difficult insight appears, one that has no analogue even in the unsual reading of Heidegger offered earlier. Contrary to what common sense would tell us, contemporary entities do not prehend each other. Appealing by way of example to the discoveries of relativity physics, Whitehead actually *defines* the simultaneity of two events in terms of their causal independence from one another. Whatever we prehend of another entity can only be that in it which has already passed away, that objectification which has finally reached us after an indefinite layover. The argument for this is unclear enough that even Whitehead's greatest disciple, Charles Hartshorne, denied for many years that it was true before later reversing himself and coming to agree with Whitehead. But however uncertain the argument, the consequences of this view are fascinating. Instead of memory being an internal mental engine that cooks and mixes left-over perceptions, perception is redefined as a form of cosmic memory, as an instrument for gathering information emitted by a past reality already dead. This also means that prehension is asymmetrical. Whatever I prehend does not actually prehend me in return, since what I prehend really no longer exists. Hartshorne claims that this is the first theory of time worthy of the name.[19] Whether that is true or not, Whitehead is at least making the effort here to elaborate a theory of time, an enterprise, we repeat, that is completely absent from Heidegger, no matter how many times he uses the words "time" or "temporality".

As has been mentioned already, there are no durable substances that persist through time; an actual entity is completely defined by its specific place with respect to all other objects. Once this changes, as it constantly does, then the actual entity is dead: for Whitehead time is nothing less than a perpetual perishing. What endures is not an individual object but a "society", a set of actual entities that combine to form what we know as a rock and retain this basic character more or less indefinitely, even if the rock-object actually dies away with the tiniest passage of time. Thus, there are social nexūs that retain a kind of identity: a social identity. But "society" is also a concept applicable to each instant. After all, even rocks and hammers are nothing like absolute integers or like prime numbers. Even the most apparently solid, irreducible objects are made up of living or non-living micro-organisms: in the case of the rock, these extend from recurrent crystal patterns all the way down to the molecules and atoms that behave like independent entities. In the case of human beings, it is easier to see that one is actually many: a moment's reflection easily shows that the end product of personal identity relies on vast networks of cardial and neural machinery, of various kinds of cells interacting in specific ways, and ultimately even on parasitic organisms inhabiting every least stretch of every living body.

Then somewhat like Leibniz (whom he so admires) Whitehead offers something like a cell theory of reality, a doctrine of interlocking machines. The difference is that for Whitehead the machines act freely, their actions in the face of their environment not foreordained in the least. This points to another major difference: for Whitehead there is no prior synchronization of the objects by God or anything else; instead, beings are freely open to each other, locked in hypersensitive mutual contact and responding to the faintest vibrations in each other's depths. There are two consequences of all this for the "process theology" inspired by Whitehead. First, freedom is real; God is all-loving, but not omnipotent. Second, not only is there no personal immortality after death, there is not even personal endurance *before* death, since every actual entity perishes immediately after its birth. The unusual ethical conclusion Whitehead draws from this is that the egoistic basis of morality is a falsehood. The Other is Other, certainly, but the I of five minutes ago is also Other, since it was not at all the same entity as the I of right now. What is primary is *eros*: the love of self is only a special case of a general enthusiasm for all of the objects surrounding us.

Before moving to our final point, it should again be emphasized that unlike Heidegger, Whitehead recognizes no special status for the conscious "as" of perception. We have already tried to push Heidegger himself in this direction, but for Whitehead no pushing is needed: the "as" is prehension and nothing more. It is Heidegger, following a long tradition, who accepts sense-data (and in practice, *visual* data) as the primary form of feeling. For Whitehead the *body* is what perceives, since visceral sensations and causal impacts are every bit as much a legitimate feeling or prehension as sense data are. It is not possible to bracket the causal origin of sensation; instead, what we call consciousness is only a late derivative of the prehensions brought about by our eardrums, optic nerves, and brain cells: sites where the root forms of causal feeling are concentrated for human beings. Again, consciousness is only a subsidiary form of the experiencing subject. According to Whitehead, neglect of this fact has caused most of the difficulties of philosophy. Whether or not he can solve these difficulties as claimed, the key to his philosophy turns out to be the same as the crucial questions we forced out of Heidegger earlier. First, what is the exact relation between the tool itself (actual entity) and the tangible surface with which it faces the world (eternal objects)? Second, how can we account for the difference between the most primitive sort of prehension and more complicated forms, such as those of bodily organs or of human consciousness itself?

Even more incredibly, Whitehead follows Heidegger (or rather, precedes him), in stumbling up against a fourfold structure. Contrary to his instincts that the actual entity should be "incurably atomic", Whitehead finds a tension in such entities between their act of unity and the specific character of all the cell-like objects that they unify. On the level of prehension, Whitehead distinguishes between the content of a proposition or perception and the relevance of the fact that we entertain it in view at all. Whitehead also agrees with Heidegger in giving the name "symbolic reference", in the broadest sense of the term, to this dual ambivalence within the entity. Like the other points of agreement we have seen between Heidegger and Whitehead, this one is striking, and leads us to consider a further series of questions.

If Heidegger's basic question is that of the meaning of being, and Whitehead's is that of the way in which individual actual entities come to birth, we are now in position to rephrase both of these questions in several other ways.

- What is the fourfold? How do its four poles manifest themselves in *different* realities?

- Regarding what is concealed from view, if it cannot appear without some residual sort of objectification, why is it that such direct making-present at least *seems* to happen?

- Regarding the force worked upon us by objects, what is the significance of the fact that appearance has both a specific content *and* hypnotizes us with a sort of imperative command?

But all of these questions are simply more specific ways of asking an even simpler question: what is an object?

4. A Fresh Look at *Zuhandenheit* (1999)

This essay was completed on 5 January, 1999 and submitted for the 1999 Annual Meeting of the Heidegger Circle at DePaul University. The submisson was rejected. The surprising fact that I spent at least two weeks working on the essay during the home stretch of my dissertation (defended successfully on 17 March), and foolishly skipped a planned first trip to Istanbul to do so (the Turkish visa was already in my passport), suggests a strong interest at the time in defending my interpretation of Heidegger among loyal specialists in his work: an enterprise abandoned long ago. It is interesting to note the vastly greater polish and self-confidence of this essay when compared with the first essay on Heidegger in this volume, composed less than two years earlier. This was probably because the end of my student career was in sight. One noteworthy point in this essay is its criticism of Heidegger's model of truth as unveiling. Also noteworthy, near the close, is my description of Heidegger as a sort of occasionalist; it was right about this time that occasionalist philosophy began to interest me greatly, though only in Egypt did I become familiar with the Islamic roots of the doctrine.

The following paper argues for an unorthodox approach to Heidegger's famous analysis of equipment. While the concept of *Zuhandenheit* (readiness-to-hand, or "tool-being") is already perhaps the most amply discussed theme in the history of Heidegger studies, it remains to be seen whether this concept has been pursued to the end on its own terms. Indeed, it is my claim that the majority of interpretations of tool-being are supported by a common prejudice, whether these interpretations be historical or structural, continental or analytic, realist or anti-realist, tool-centered or language-centered. The congenital bias of all such approaches lies in assuming that the analysis of equipment serves as a limited account of one specific phenomenon: namely, the human *use* of tools. Now, this may have been precisely what Heidegger intended. Even so, what is of most interest is not the content of Heidegger's self-understanding, but the unforeseen direction in which contemporary ontology is forced to travel as a result of his tool-analysis. There should be nothing surprising about this claim. Numerous passages can be found in which Heidegger tells us that the historian must focus on what was left in the background of a philosophy rather than on what it specifically brought to light. Of course, even if he had said the opposite we would still have a right to ignore his advice; we need not seek Heidegger's permission to read him in such and such a way. His insight into tool-being is a discovery that belongs to the ages, and is arguably the pivot point of twentieth century philosophy. We can no more expect that he achieved transparency as to all its features than we can expect Aristotle to have foreseen every future conception of substance, or Lavoisier to have exhausted in advance every feature of the chemical structure of water.

To repeat, the central claim of this paper is that Heidegger's tool-analysis should not be read as a limited account of human productive or technical activity. Instead, it turns out that with the theory of equipment Heidegger gives us an insight of overwhelming scope, one that cannot be restricted to "tools" in the narrow sense of the term, and ultimately cannot even be restricted to the sphere of human life. The discussion of tool-being provides us with nothing less than a metaphysics of reality, in spite of the understandable abuse that Heidegger and his successors have heaped on the term "metaphysics". I will return to this issue at the conclusion. For now, two basic steps in the argument can be itemized:

1) The tool-analysis is unsuccessful if we read it as saying that nothing exists outside the contexture of human meanings and projects. In fact, it establishes just the opposite. The tool-being of the hammer is not a technical or linguistic practice, but a capital

X that forever recedes from all contact with human meaning-fulness. The tool isn't "used"; it *is*. In this way, the tool-analysis steers us not toward an improved account of human Dasein, but toward a theory of objects themselves.

2) The discussion of *Zuhandenheit* cannot possibly be limited, as is often done, to a recognized catalog of wooden and metallic hardware. Whatever Heidegger's intentions may have been, his analysis of tool-being does not apply to tools as opposed to entities which are not tools. The description of equipment does not serve as a regional ontology that could be limited to the order of hatchets, drills, and pulleys. Instead, tool-being is the name for a fundamental dualism that rips through the heart of everything that is: not just tools in the limited sense, but also plants, animals, numbers, machines, rocks, and even people.

These two claims make up the heart of the argument. If they can be established, it will not be surprising if other familiar cross-roads in Heidegger's thought can also be seen in a rather different light. With this slight shift of viewpoint, as with any pair of colored lenses or toy telescope, certain portions of the landscape will seem less troubling than before, though others will appear more mysterious than ever. For simplicity's sake it is possible to limit the remaining claims of this paper to five additional points. To prepare the way for what follows, I now conclude these introductory remarks with a point-by-point overview, so as to suppress the always distracting role of surprise. The first two points are the ones just itemized:

Point 1 is that the theory of equipment is not an account of human practical comportment, but an ontology of entities or objects themselves. I will use the word "objects" interchangeably with "beings" or "entities", despite Heidegger's own restriction of the term "object" to the pejorative sense of "mere correlate of a representation".

Point 2 is that the tool-analysis does not just cover a distinct class of entities sold by hardware merchants. Heidegger's argument necessarily encompasses all entities, regardless of whether he *meant* to cast so wide a net. Equipment is global; beings are tool-beings. Having repeated these initial arguments, some further implications immediately follow.

Point 3. Just as the "tool" must be regarded as a universal concept in Heidegger, the same is true of what might be called the "broken tool". Heidegger's vivid discussion of failed equipment is misread if we view it as an account of special moments of rupture that occur from time to time. In fact, his insight into malfunctioning equipment tells us nothing special about shattered chisels and flat tires that is not true of all other things as well. The oscillation between tool and broken tool occurs in each entity at every moment. Readiness-to-hand and presence-at-hand are not terms that describe certain objects or situations as opposed to others. Instead, they mark a global dualism that saturates every least corner of the universe. The rift between tool and tool "as" tool cannot be pinpointed in specific examples alone.

Point 4 is more surprising. Namely, we cannot restrict this as-structure to cases of human comportment, whatever our opinions about the relative success or failure of Heidegger's 1929/30 remarks on animal life. The as-structure can indeed be found in animals, for the simple reason that it can already be found in mushrooms, trees, and inanimate rock. Human consciousness is a far more specific reality than the "as". Since the time of Kant, most philosophers who have tried to make any definitive statement about reality beyond the human pale have been regarded as renegade cosmologists if not out-and-out cranks. Be that as it may, I hold that Heidegger's tool-being drives us in precisely this direction, toward the concealed infrastructure of the perceived world.

Point 5. The gap between tool-being and its presence is *absolute*. There is no way of approaching equipment directly, not even asymptotically and by degrees. Whatever comes to presence of a thing is *ipso facto* something different from the withdrawn *being* of that thing. This leads to a slight shift in Heidegger's question of truth. The point is not only that some residual negative will continue to haunt any presence; the problem is that no uncovering movement can ever get us the least bit closer to the thing at all. While the notion of *aletheia* or unveiling is certainly preferable to truth as correctness, it fails to do justice to the utter incommensurability of readiness-to-hand and presence-at-hand. These are two utterly distinct ontological dimensions: one is never convertible into the other, not even approximately. As a result, Heidegger would need to replace unveiling with yet another conception of truth, but never does this.

Point 6. Not only does Heidegger fail to discuss "tools" as a specific reality opposed to "non-tools": more than this, he fails to discuss *any* specific subject matter. For all his thousands of pages, it will turn out that Heidegger is a thinker of almost staggering pre-Socratic simplicity. Whatever his attempts at sensitive analyses of concrete subject matter, his ostensibly detailed accounts soon implode back into a universal dualism of *Zu-* and *Vorhandenheit*, tool and broken tool. The celebrated analysis of time merely repeats the simple reversal between subterranean equipment and its sparkling visible surface, and would hold good even if what we know as "time" were forever frozen in its tracks. By the same token, Heidegger's discussion of space holds equally well for non-spatial entities; his account of theoretical comportment has no more to do with theory than with the laziest forms of "tarrying"; and the influential artwork essay never manages to show how the strife in the artwork is different from the kind that already circulates through every pore of reality. In short, Heidegger excels at collapsing every particular subject matter into a formidable ontological *fundament*, which I would argue is the true meaning of the phrase "fundamental ontology". But he does not succeed at mapping the contours of any specific reversal or *metabole* in the cosmos, which I hold would be the task of his abortive "metontology", relevant for far more than the stated themes of ethics and sexual difference.

Point 7 amounts to a sort of final summary. If the preceding points hold, at least three unfamiliar philosophical problems emerge from Heidegger's analyses. First, if there are always two dimensions in every entity at all times, it will not be a question of which has priority over the other, but of how both are *inscribed* in one another. Second, if Heidegger's attempts to discuss specific zones of reality such as time, theory, tools, and artworks do not succeed, is there any glimmer in his writings of a real metontology that would be capable of tackling these themes? Third and last, if the tools themselves are incapable of coming to presence through the as-structure through even a *partial* unveiling, how is it that they have any effect on the kingdom of presence at all? I will make no effort to discuss these serious questions, aiming only to show that they must be clarified by means of a *metaphysical* approach, even if this term currently enjoys less prestige in both analytic and Continental philosophy than at almost any time in its history. If metaphysics must remains dead as ontotheology (in which one privileged object is held to explain or exemplify the others) metaphysics as a speculative theory on the nature of ultimate reality may soon enter a new heyday as an ironic result of Heidegger's critical efforts. Having offered this initial taste of the main features of the argument, I will try to develop them in as much detail as the present format allows.

* * *

We can begin with the famous scenario of equipment itself. Let's imagine that Nietzsche is at his table in Sils-Maria one morning, at work on the manuscript of *Zarathustra* II. As the famous photos attest, he is surrounded by a variety of austere daily objects: bed, washstand, chair, floor, walls, and table. He is wearing shoes rather than touching the floor with naked feet, breathing freely in the cool mountain air rather than coughing in the fumes of a mine shaft. He is stationed amidst these objects in a distinct way, his life determined by the whole of this situation. Nonetheless, the air is swarming with micro-organisms both helpful and harmful. The sun rises slowly, bombarding the air with photons, ultra-violet rays, and other entities not yet discovered. In the world beyond Nietzsche's room, certain people continue to live while others have already died; certain governments flourish while others fall into languid decay. In short, this moment is no different from each of the moments that all of us live, no different even from the present moment. In accordance with the analysis of tool-being, how should it be interpreted?

Any reader of Heidegger will at least be able to say how *not* to interpret it. Namely, the situation should never be described as follows: Nietzsche sits in absolute physical space, surrounded by chemical agglomerates of wood and cloth that are formed after the fact into specific useful shapes; he is irradiated by material particles from the sun and also socially determined by a comprehensive list of true politico-economic facts. This is the "ontic" approach, and it is precisely what Martin Heidegger was born to annihilate. But what alternative does Heidegger offer?

One answer to this question asserts that he describes the room by stripping it of all things-in-themselves. To speak of any one of these things (table, chair, photon) in isolation from human Dasein would be to reduce it to an independent present-at-hand material. What comes prior to the thing in isolation is the thing in its usefulness, in its projection upon a set of human possibilities. This would be called the thing in its readiness-to-hand. While the independent hammer is nothing but a mere slab of metal sitting around in space, the same hammer in Dasein's hands becomes action for a purpose. As this reading would have it, independence from Dasein equals presence-at-hand, while intimate connection with Dasein is equivalent to readiness-at-hand. I oppose this reading completely.

Each of the objects in Nietzsche's room rumbles in its depths, unleashing powerful forces in its ceaseless duels and friendships with the others. The bulky table sustains a sheet of paper that compresses the table ever so lightly in return. The legs of the chair dig into the floor as if to wound it, ungrateful for the support they receive, thankless toward the ground that stops them from plummeting to the center of the earth. Photons ricochet off Nietzsche's pale hands like bullets, reflected in an instant toward the coldest reaches of distant space. It is only because the things act in this way, only because they collide with and caress each other, bolster and undermine each other, that Nietzsche can ever "use" them. To say that Nietzsche's chair is serviceable for sitting, or that the sun is useful for helping him to see, is already to offer a *theory* about these objects. None of these statements touches the primary reality, where the sun in its being puts table-being and bed-being under assault with its radiant thermal energies.

One way of creating a theory about the sun, of reducing it to a present-at-hand object, is to describe it in terms of nuclear reactions. But defining the sun as equipment-for-warming-me, or as tool-for-illuminating-my-sky, is just another theory about it, another reduction of the sun to *Vorhandenheit*. The sun isn't effective because I use it. Rather, it can only be used because it is capable of an effect, of inflicting some sort of blow upon reality. The sun isn't "used"; it *is*. The same is equally true of table and floor and bed. It is not my enjoyment of these objects that first conjures them into being. Instead, I always find myself deployed amidst a specific geography of objects, each of them withdrawing from view into a dark primal integrity that neither our theories nor our practices can ever fully exhaust.

The best way to sum up this difficult point might be as follows. Some readers, perhaps including Heidegger himself, hold that the world in itself is a kind of vacant lot filled with bland present-at-hand materials that would need to be jazzed up by an encounter with human beings. The universe would be a pile of neutral material slabs, with human reality alone capable of adding some drama to an otherwise dreary field of colorless atoms. The subject of the tool-analysis would be nothing but the way in which Dasein superimposes an alluring grid of activities and moods onto piles of vacuous inert matter that swarm through empty space.

But things are quite the contrary: in fact, we have no idea what physical mass really is. There is nothing "in itself" about the concept of matter: this is a sheer human theoretical invention. Against what has been claimed, it is not Dasein which liberates the world from mere *Vorhandenheit*. Rather, insofar as Dasein comes into contact with something, it immediately *converts it* into presence-at-hand. The readiness-to-hand of a hammer is not primarily technical, social, or linguistic, but primarily ontological. This can be seen somewhat more clearly, though no more truly, if we consider kinds of equipment not created by Dasein. Nietzsche relies, for example, on the solidity of the earth. He depends upon the breathability of the air, the might of the ozone layer, and the convenient distance of the earth from the sun, perfect for his species. In none of these cases would we confidently assert: "Oh, the sun is nothing but equipment for warming and brightening; the ozone is sheer usefulness for blocking dangerous rays, and nothing more". These statements are all *theories* that are far from exhausting the subterranean reality of these objects with which each of us dwells in every moment. In fact we have no real idea what the floor is, what the solar rays are, what atoms are, what matter is. Any thoughts we might have about these issues would be no better than a present-at-hand approximation of reality, a *Vorhandenheit* for which we have only ourselves to blame. What really lies beneath our feet at each moment is not a usefulness, but an inaccessible netherworld that we can use *because* it is there. It is the Empire of the Capital X.

Tool-being is not a human reality to be explained in terms of technical or linguistic background practices. Rather, it is that which withdraws from all human access, that which all practical and theoretical explanations can only feebly reflect, due to their permanent distance from the tool-beings themselves. Sun, bed, floor, and table all unleash their personalities to create the total environment of Nietzsche's room. In the first place, Nietzsche obviously never notices *all* of these factors; in the second place, even his invisible practical reliance on such objects in no way exhausts their being. The tool-analysis is not primarily concerned with the human use of tools simply because human praxis stands from the outset at the mercy of a system of objects cutting and breaking and burning one another. It is from out of this system of the world that theory *and* practice both arise. Whatever Heidegger may have intended the theory of equipment to mean, it ends up telling us much more than "practice comes before theory". The tool-analysis is really about the two-faced nature of the tools themselves. On the one hand they are locked in the silent drama of force-against-force that generates a new world at every moment. On the other hand they emerge into view, though always by way of a specific perspective.

By definition, the tools must already exceed these perspectives. The sun is clearly not reducible to what Nietzsche or the rest of us experience of it, or even what inanimate objects undergo in the presence of it. The sun has countless further traits that none of the astral entities currently in the neighborhood is competent to unlock. Thus I would argue that there is a frank *realism* at work from the first step of the tool-analysis, whether Heidegger meant this to happen or not. Yet it is an exceedingly strange sort of realism, since it would have to regard every concept of particles, waves, matter, and causation as mere present-at-hand theories. The reality of tool-being recedes behind any specific incarnation of itself, giving it more in common with a monad than with a typical handyman's device. Bypassing this historical comparison for lack of time, Point 1 of the argument has now been reached. The tool-analysis tells us not only about Nietzsche's practical comportment in the room. More than this, it informs us that the floor has a being on which he is already dependent, as do each of the other entities in what we might call the Sils-Maria Network, all of them helping to compose the present moment of his life. This is Point Number 1: the tool-analysis tells us something about the tools themselves.

The next point quickly follows: "tool-being" is universal. We cannot restrict this term to certain objects at the expense of others. It is not just hammers, tables, and sun that function in a certain way before we ever see them. The same is true even of a useless grain of dust. If Nietzsche is distracted by this dust-grain as it drifts past the windowpane, his perception of it does not exhaust the dust in its being. Neither does he exhaust its reality by encountering it *unconsciously*, since if it runs up against his skin and causes a severe allergic reaction, the dust still harbors additional qualities from which perhaps only a cat or a spider could suffer. The tool-being of the dust does not come from its human usefulness or lack thereof, but from the fact that the brute reality of this dust exceeds any of its *particular* effects.

The tool-analysis, to repeat, does not give us information about a certain class of entities that serves as means to an end. It tells us instead that no entity is exhausted by its series of encounters with other entities, since there is always more to the entity than it shows. If we recognize that "tool" means "reality" rather than "usefulness", there should no longer be any compunction about saying that human Dasein is also ready-to-hand, despite Heidegger's explicit statements to the contrary. To say that human beings are *zuhanden* does not mean that we successfully manipulate them in Machiavellian fashion. It only signifies that the reality of each of us is something quite different from what we or anyone else will ever be able to know about it. If not for this, the laborious work of introspection or full-blown psychoanalysis would be totally unnecessary. Each of our subtlest motives and talents and limitations would be easily visible at a glance, and we would not invest a lifetime exploring and defining them. Thus, even human being is tool-being. Perhaps Nietzsche is treated kindly in Sils-Maria, or perhaps he is ruthlessly exploited by his landlord and treacherous friends. In either case, Nietzsche is tool-being to an equal degree.

Tool-being is not a quantitative unit of manipulability that increases or decreases depending on how much an entity is being handled. Rather, it makes up a full unchanging half of reality, everywhere and at all times: namely, the half that has not reversed into some sort of perspectival presence-at-hand for an observer. Heidegger had already shown us that the hammer has two faces, readiness-to-hand and presence-at-hand. It now turns out that the same is true of a dust-grain, a person, and *a fortiori* of a dog, a sunflower, and an artwork. All of these objects are marked by a contrast between their subterranean reality and the series of phenomenal surfaces they generate in our encounter with them. This is Point Number 2: the tool-analysis holds good for any entity whatsoever, not just for "useful" ones. It is for this reason that I would argue that the best historical analogy for tool-being is not to be found in Aristotle's *poiesis*. The comparison with Aristotle succeeds only if Heidegger's tool-analysis is really describing the production of independently standing products. I have argued that this claim stems from an overly literal reading of hammers, and that the analysis can never be restricted to productive implements. By my reading, even a tree is tool-being although it is certainly not "produced" in Aristotle's sense. To repeat, the tool-analysis holds good for everything, not just for a blacksmith's production *as opposed* to the praxis of an orator or statesman. It has turned out to be an ontology of objects in general, not a taxonomy of human comportment.

This brings us to the next point, which follows quite easily if the previous one is accepted. Heidegger's discussion of failed equipment is not only an account of how reliable objects cease to work. Like the discussion of the tool, that of the broken tool has a universal ontological scope. Just as the tool doesn't always mean "useful", the broken tool doesn't always mean "broken". For Heidegger, when equipment fails then its prior unthematic function comes to view; it is liberated to some degree from its invisible potency in the world and comes to light "as" what it is. The same is true of theory, which might be regarded as a *deliberate* subversion of equipment so as to bring the thing to light in its prior undisclosed reality.

In each case the movement is the same: that which used to be hidden and merely efficacious now exposes its visceral contours in the light of day. But these are not special, privileged moments. If the broken tool exposes the reality of the thing, so does the masterfully constructed, prize-winning tool that never fails us in the least. Even flawless equipment usually does not just vanish into the invisible infrastructure of the city, but at least shines with a particular color, or emits a characteristic hum, or vibrates noticeably. Equally so, it is not just theory out of all the human comportments that liberates the thing from its shadowy depth. The same occurs even in the laziest tarrying alongside objects. Even the lethargic slacker does not drift in a coma through some unconscious underworld, but sees things to some degree "as" what they are. He clearly sees that tree over there, though he never puts in the work to learn very much about it. Then even the most atheoretical moments have already liberated at least some features of an object into the clearing. In short, the whole of the world is a constant interplay between these structures of tool and broken tool. We have seen that these terms refer not just to hammers and screwdrivers, but to all entities in their two-faced reversal between underground effect and visible profile. Any object that gets noticed at all is marked by a reversal or *metabole* into "broken tool", as Heidegger tells us himself in *History of the Concept of Time*.

This is the place to address one possible objection, however briefly. It might be thought that individual entities, oscillating between tool-being and the as-structure, are merely a superficial foreground. It might be said that the discussion of specific objects is nothing better than a starting point, and that what must be done next is to pass gradually from these objects into their "ground". From the concern with specific entities, we must cross over to the care in which concern is grounded, from care to ecstatic temporality in general, and from there to the clearing-lightening event of appropriation in which time temporalizes. Intermediate steps can be added wherever you please. But I would argue that these sorts of movements in Heidegger's work are valuable only as tactical devices that counter any attempt to grasp his successive terms in a present-at-hand way. Being may not be a specific being, but it is the very *reversal* into specific beings. The flight from objects into their ever deeper grounds is a useful strategy only as long as objects are mistaken for present-at-hand material clods. There is nothing inherently ontic about a hammer or a toothbrush. There are only ontic *interpretations* of these items, which wrongly reduce them to physical masses employed after the fact for daily chores. But Heidegger's tool-analysis has already taken things to a deeper level than this. The point is not to move as far away from objects as possible, but to move as far from the unfettered dominance of *Vorhandenheit* as possible.

There follows Point 3: the two-sided relation between tool and broken tool is a global structure, equally present whether the objects in question are literally broken or instead flawlessly operative. We might simply call this the relation between tool and tool "as" tool. Every square inch of Heidegger's thought is saturated with this relation: it is the atom from which his philosophy is built. It might be wondered whether there is any way to split this atom so as to reveal its internal workings in even greater detail. For now, we need not attempt any such thing, but can simply pass on to the next point.

One of the most frequent ways to speak of the difference between the tool and the as-structure is to equate it with the difference between causality and perception. Beneath the hammer as a visible metallic figure, there is the hammer in its causal impact on the boards and houses with which it is now in contact. I would argue that the truth is stranger than this: in fact, even physical causation should be placed on the level of the as-structure. If the claim is rejected, this will be due to the understandable tendency to equate the as-structure with consciousness, and even with human consciousness more narrowly. Insofar as a chair does not perceive the floor on which it rests, there is supposedly no "as" at work in the inanimate realm. My contention is that Heidegger's account of the as-structure places it on a far more universal plane than he would wish. The "as" turns out to be far more basic than human consciousness.

Let's consider the case of a falling leaf, which runs up against a stone wall and is thereby blocked in its motion. I do not claim that the leaf "perceives" the wall, but do claim that the leaf encounters this entity "as" a wall nonetheless. It certainly does not encounter it as a flame, for that would be to burn; nor does it encounter it as a whirling blade, for that would amount to being instantly shredded. The leaf is not conscious as far as we know, but it does react to each entity in the world in vastly different ways; it confronts them in some primitive way "as" what they are. Note that the encounter between leaf and wall is just as perspectivally limited as any human comportment. By falling after it touches the wall, the leaf does not exhaust the wall's reality. It does not shatter against it, nor does it engage in chemical reaction with the materials that bind the stones together. Other entities might well do these things, thereby invoking forces in the wall that the leaf never remotely touches. This is the real meaning of the "as": one entity always encounters another only from a certain standpoint, only liberates *some* of its energies. But in addition to this primitive "as", Heidegger implies the existence of an enhanced or turbo-charged version of the as-structure, one that he would deny even to highly intelligent animals such as dolphins and monkeys. In this connection, he often says things like "the animal may encounter its food, but not 'as' food; only Dasein does this". But with statements of this sort, Heidegger merely asserts a gradation in forms of the as-structure without actually establishing one.

Again, I will grant that human consciousness belongs to an entirely different order from the encounter of a leaf with a wall. What I will deny is that Heidegger (or anyone else) can account for this difference by means of the as-structure. In practice, the "as" can refer only to the difference between the rich tool-being of a thing and the necessarily limited profile of it that is encountered by another entity. This rudimentary difference can indeed be found in the human perception of a wall, but is already present in the merest leaf's collision with a wall. There may be a special dignity of human consciousness, but it needs a more complicated treatment than mere appeal to the "as", which exists even in the inanimate realm.

This is none other than Point Number 4: the as-structure is not only of human relevance, but also belongs to inanimate reality. The custom is to distinguish between causality and perception, invisibility and visibility. In fact, the only relevant distinction is that between actuality and relation. Bearing this in mind, it becomes clear why even causality must be a form of the as-structure: tool-being retreats even behind the drama of cause and effect, holding most of its forces in reserve at any given moment, behind any causal encounter.

This leads us directly to the next theme on the list: Heidegger's theory of truth. We can begin with the permanent contribution he has made in this regard. By opposing the notion of unveiling to the tradition of truth as correctness, Heidegger draws a legitimate consequence from his critique of presence-at-hand. Truth is not correctness, simply because it is impossible to mirror reality exhaustively with theoretical propositions or any sort of as-structure at all. The content of consciousness and the content of reality never match up exactly; there will always be some residual depth to the entity behind anything we might be able to say about it. Truth never gives us the thing in the flesh, but only unveils it by degrees. So far, so good.

But where the saving power is, there too lies the danger. Against all expectations, truth as unveiling is at odds with itself from the very moment of its birth. The danger arises insofar as Heidegger is forced to put the as-structure to two distinct and incompatible uses. On the one hand, all experience is experience of a thing "as" something specific. Even those who disagree with my claim that the "as" can be found at the inanimate level will probably agree that human experience *per se* is characterized by the as-structure. Nietzsche at his desk in Sils-Maria makes use of the unveiling "as", and so does the drunkard outside who is being hauled to a Swiss courtroom. But Heidegger wants to use the "as" both as a universal structure *and* as a measuring stick to determine which sorts of comportment are closer to the things than other comportments are. Let's say that the drunkard is being dragged past a tree on his way to jail. This tree not only has an unthematic effect on the poor man by invisibly refreshing the air he breathes: he also sees the tree, in whatever hazy or mediocre way. Now, it is possible to observe the tree in an even more lucid way than the drunkard's perception of a mere blurry shape; perhaps Nietzsche succeeds in doing this when he looks outside to observe the ensuing commotion. A maverick botanist might be in the vicinity and be led to pay even closer attention to the tree.

And if Nietzsche gets into just the right mood, he might be willing to go even further than the botanist, and somehow grasp the tree in its being.

But even if it is granted that each of these stages tells us a bit more about the tree, the as-structure cannot possibly be the mechanism for differentiating them. The tree in its tool-being stands at an unbridgeable distance from any manifestation of itself to other entities, no matter what form this manifestation assumes. The blurry shape observed by the drunkard is undeniably tree "as" tree. The same is true when the botanist declares it to be "Norway spruce", or when Nietzsche emerges from his room to meditate on the eternal recurrence while gazing at its fateful branches. The blurry tree-image and the ontological insight into the tree both see the tree explicitly rather than relying unconsciously on its effects. They both liberate the tree from its tool-being into the as-structure. The problem is that we cannot say that the botanist or the ontologist sees the tree *even more* "as" what it is than the drunkard does. The reason is simple: by definition, the tree in its tool-being can never come to presence at all. As soon as the tree appears, it is already loitering in the sphere of presence-at-hand rather than existing patiently in its own subterranean depth. No property of the tree is any closer to its permanently withdrawn reality than any other. For this reason, contrary to our first impressions of the concept, the as-structure cannot function by degrees. Surprisingly, the concept is utterly binary: there are only tool-being and the as-structure, and not different gradations of the "as".

This is not meant as an argument for relativism. There has to be a sense in which the botanist's insight is a far greater knowledge than the pre-scientific blur seen by the condemned prisoner. But the distance between them is not covered by getting "closer" to the thing, as if one moment were "less" veiled than the other. In the end, both experiences are shadowed by an absolute veil, by an infinite inaccessibility of the tree in its genuine *Vollzug* or performance. An infinitely distant place remains infinitely removed no matter how far we travel. The properties of the tree that are successively unearthed by the botanist are completely incommensurable with the infernal tree-being that withdraws from all perception, and ultimately from all causation. Truth cannot possibly be *aletheia*, since nothing ever manages to be unveiled, not even a little bit. Everything that was beneath the veil at the beginning remains beneath the veil at the conclusion; nothing ever passes from one side of this rift to the other. A different model of truth and of theoretical comportment is necessary, one that I cannot claim to offer in anything more than the negative sense just described. This is Point Number Five: nothing ever becomes unveiled. Thus, the true mechanism by which tool-being and presence are related remains a mystery.

The sixth and penultimate point may be the most interesting to some listeners, though for reasons of time it can receive only a hasty overview. My claim here is that Heidegger never tells us about any concrete subject matter at all, but merely replays his structural coupling of tool and broken tool *ad nauseam* in every possible context. This will have to be shown loosely, in connection with a rather brief remark on Heidegger's concept of time. Despite the heavy technical argumentation surrounding the ecstatic analyses, the upshot of these analyses is so profound and so simple that it can be easily explained even to novices in philosophy.

Given Heidegger's status as a ruthless critic of presence, it is only natural that his theory of time should also be a formidable critique of the *present*. It is not that Nietzsche sits in his room here and now, with the table and the chair and the sunbeams also present here and now. Instead, Nietzsche finds himself in a situation of temporal ambiguity. In what does this ambiguity consist? Table and chair and sunbeam do not just sit there as bland inert masses; each of them is already enmeshed in ontological crisis. When we consider Nietzsche's status in the room, we find that even "The Crucified" cannot just dream up whatever world he pleases, as if *ex nihilo*: he already finds himself trapped in a viscous atmosphere of table, clothing, sunlight, and air. This system of objects, into which Nietzsche is already thrown, *is* the "past" of Heidegger's ecstases. But by the same token, this system of objects is not an obvious unequivocal lump. It is there *for* Nietzsche, all of it beneficial or deleterious for his own specific projects. The room might have an utterly different impact on any of Nietzsche's visitors, to say nothing of how futile it will seem for the aged moth slowly perishing on his windowsill. This way in which the given entities of Nietzsche's thrownness appear in a specific light in accordance with his own constitution as a distinct entity, is the "future" of Heidegger's ecstases. The "present" is simply the site where these counterposed dimensions fold into one another. Heidegger's temporality is nothing other than this, the fateful reversal between the thing in its projection and the same thing in the secluded headquarters of its being.

But does this really have anything to do with time? Let's suppose that we had the power of gods to freeze time in its tracks, and perform this thought experiment on Sils-Maria to see what happens (it is only Bergson who denies that time can ever be reduced to freeze frames; there is nothing in Heidegger to prevent it). The experiment has begun, and time has ceased its flow. Nietzsche is now frozen in place over his manuscript, while all the objects that crowd his room are fixated in place. Are Nietzsche and the objects now reduced to the single dimension of presence? Does the triple ecstatic analysis disappear once times has been halted? Surprisingly, not at all. Even now Nietzsche remains thrown into one specific environment and no other. And even now the objects in this environment are not just neutral crystalline solids, but are plugged into all the projections of the Nietzsche-system, and appear in a different and even more sorrowful way to the dying moth. The ecstatic analysis still works.

The conclusion: Heidegger's celebrated analysis of time does not give us time at all, since it works just as well for a situation stripped of any temporal characteristics. To say that it deserves the name "time" insofar as it is the "ground" for ontic clock-time is invalid, since it is actually the ground for *everything* ontic, and has no special intimate connection with time that it does not also have with space or with theory. It cannot be objected that Heidegger would oppose such a reading of time as a "sequence of now-points". For what Heidegger attacks is not the now-points, but the *sequence*: the belief that time is composed of present-at-hand instants that can find a liberation from presence-at-hand only *outside* of themselves. The key Heideggerian discovery, as Levinas puts it, is that "an instant is not one lump; it is articulated". But Levinas is also right to view Heidegger as an occasionalist, since for him the ambiguous strands linking all portions of an instant supersede any theory of how *different* instants are connected with one another. Heidegger shows no interest in this latter theme at all, unlike Bergson.

This is Point Number 6, intimately related to the previous one. There the problem was that no moment of unveiling could be distinguished as more or less unveiled than any other, so that there was no way to discern between varying degrees of truth. Here, the analogous problem is that there is no way to distinguish between time and that which is not time. Although further argument here would take us too far afield, there also turns out to be no difference between space and that which is not space, or the artwork and that which is not an artwork. In each case, a zone of reality is defined only in terms of the relation between a prior reality (tool-being) and the way in which this reality is liberated into view (the as-structure). Each sphere of being is described as a particular sort of *Entfernung* ("de-distancing") or *Entleben* ("de-living"), but scratch the surface of his accounts of time or space or art, and it will be seen that they hold good for everything under the sun, and by no means do they clarify their objects as *specific* realities. It doesn't take an artwork to create strife in Heidegger's world, and as we have seen, it is fruitless to suggest that the artwork is unique in giving us strife "as" strife. This is nothing but a further attempt to smuggle a measuring-stick function into an as-structure that is permanent, universal, uniform everywhere at every moment. In short, wherever Heidegger turns he is unable to serve up anything more than a repetitive theory of how transparency is forever haunted by opacity. While this must happen very differently in the cases of a Greek temple and a Chaldean temple, he never tells us how. Even in the seductive descriptions of the fourfold, we learn nothing about the mirror-play in a jug or bridge that would be any different from the mirror-play in a mountain or an anvil. There is no metontology in Heidegger, only "notes toward" a metontology.

I pass directly to the conclusion of this paper. From the reading of Heidegger offered here, three basic philosophical problems could be said to arise. First, there is the need for a better account of the *relation* between the integral tool-being of a thing and the manifold profiles that it offers to us and to all other entities. It is not just a question of trying to determine whether practice or theory has primary status. The rather different question that now emerges is how any trace of the tool can be inscribed in the realm of the as-structure, which is supposed to be utterly incommensurable with it. Second, we can also ask the converse. Given any particular perception or theoretical account of an object, how can we "deepen" our experience of that object if it has proven impossible ever to advance a single step closer toward the object itself? If no gradual approach via unveiling is possible, how can we avoid a free-for-all in which every vague grasp of a thing "as" something is interchangeable with even the profoundest breakthroughs into it? How is it possible to account for the expansion of human knowledge if we abandon not only the bodily presence of the thing itself, but also the asymptotic

5. Bruno Latour, King of Networks (1999)

My reading of Latour's books began in February 1998 at the recommendation of a Swiss acquaintance named Felix Stalder, then a doctoral candidate at the University of Toronto. We had met in Toronto the previous month when I lectured there twice on the Heidegger-McLuhan relationship. The following year, someone requested that I give a talk on Latour's philosophy at DePaul University, and this finally occurred on 16 April, 1999. Professor Bill Martin was in attendance that day and recommended that I send a copy of the lecture to Latour himself. I did so, and thus began a rewarding correspondence with Latour that continued during the years that followed.

In the spring of 1996, *Social Text* published Alan Sokal's infamous hoax article "Transgressing the Boundaries: Toward a Transformative Hermeneutics of Quantum Gravity".[20] Posing as a postmodern critique of the natural sciences, the article was actually an ingenious Trojan Horse, designed to mock the positions it seemingly defended. Whatever else can be said about Sokal's article, as a work of parody it is little short of a master-piece. Indeed, it must be counted as the finest intellectual prank of the decade even by those of us who find several of our favorite authors among its victims. As you will remember, the article immediately caused a great stir, with full exposés appearing in the pages of *The New York Times*, *The Nation*, and other mass-circulation periodicals. Residing that spring in the university town of Iowa City, I was delighted by the news, and immediately summoned a handful of close friends to a dimly lit tavern where we enjoyed a round of celebratory drinks.[21] Despite our misgivings about Sokal's pompous gloating and hamfisted philo-sophical sermons, he was the man of the hour in our hearts. However, this state of affairs did not last for long. The brilliant poker-faced mood of the *Social Text* article soon gave way to

Sokal's preachy public crusade against relativism, one no different in many ways from those found in the facile newspaper columns of George Will and Arianna Huffington. We were also subjected to the tiresome spectacle of Sokal touting his own Leftist credentials against those of *rive gauche* postmodernists, as a tedious debate between public figures soon erupted ("I'm more radical than you are."; "No, it is I who am the true radical, and I have taught in Central America to prove it.") But worst of all, Sokal's parody was later to serve as the basis for an insipid book-length survey of French philosophy, co-authored with Belgian physicist Jean Bricmont, bearing the cornpone title *Fashionable Nonsense*.[22] Among its primary targets were Lacan, Kristeva, Irigaray, Baudrillard, Deleuze/Guattari, Virilio, Lyotard, and Derrida. These names are familiar enough to those in the room today, but among Sokal's whipping boys and whipping girls was an additional name that was less familiar to me at the time, and is presumably still unfamiliar to most of you: Bruno Latour.

My talk today is meant not only as a basic overview of Latour's work, but as an *enthusiastic* overview. For numerous reasons, it seems to me that he is not grouped so easily with the other figures on the postmodern hit list, whether you think *they* deserve to be there or not. Far younger than his fellow targets, Latour seems to me to represent a new phase of French philosophy that is in many respects at odds with the more familiar one. Although this does not automatically mean that Latour succeeds in trumping his older French contemporaries, it does mean that he and they cannot be slain with a single sword, as Sokal lazily attempts to do. Contrary to Sokal's assertions, Latour does not endorse the anti-realist and holistic theory of reality that is often found in recent French thought, but criticizes these positions severely from the outset. Most importantly, he does not propose that science is socially constituted by power relations or figurative linguistic strategies. Instead, Latour's universe is populated with countless human and non-human *actors*. Political power acts upon us and textual rhetoric acts upon us, but so do cement walls, icebergs, tobacco fields, and poisonous snakes. Prior to any distinction between animate and inanimate, between "naturally real" and "socially produced", the world is a duel of genuine discrete entities. In this way, philosophy is subtly transformed into what Latour calls an "actor-network theory", a term to be discussed again shortly.

In the meantime, a final word on the peripheral question of the *Social Text* prank will lead us directly to a reflection on the most widespread misunderstanding of Latour's work in this country. It must be admitted that Sokal's article does everything a good parody should do. It keeps a straight face for dozens of pages rather than going for easy laughs. It avoids silly exaggerations of that which it mimics, and confines itself to copying *real* stylistic quirks of postmodern thought; it foregoes obvious punch lines and simply plays its role to the hilt. For this reason alone was it able to pass undetected through the watchdogs at *Social Text*. But what, exactly, does the article succeed in mocking? Why were my friends and I so eager to salute it with whiskey and champagne?

I would suggest that Sokal's article has primarily the following virtues. Above all else, it rips the slavish protocol of academic discourse, which seems to have reached its ironic zenith in the supposedly liberating context of postmodernism. For example, the style of Sokal's article is itself nearly unreadable due to the inclusion of 109 footnotes, most of them utterly pointless. Would a parody with *no* footnotes ever have been accepted? You be the judge. In another hilarious feature of the hoax, Sokal's brief thirty-three-page article was somehow allowed to past muster with the editors in spite of an insufferable twelve-page Bibliography. The simplest criteria of readability and clear style should have been enough to earn him an instant rejection letter. Meanwhile, rampant flattery and bootlicking hold court in every paragraph, while smug academic jargon such as "problematize" and "relativize" is scattered throughout the parody's pages with facile ease. Worst of all, not a single harsh word is uttered against any of the great academic stars of French or American postmodernism. This sort of obsequiousness, which often masks itself as modesty or gratitude, really has the effect of rendering those of high academic position almost untouchable, thereby cementing the continued existence of cliquish enclaves that would make a high school cheerleading squad proud. Instead of the Wild West atmosphere that original thought needs in order to thrive, Sokal's article only replicates the cynical maneuvers of the social chessboard, as when *Social Text* editor Stanley Aronowitz is himself quoted in the article's epigraph.

All of this is highly entertaining, and fully deserves the celebratory toast that we dedicated to it. But Sokal is strangely convinced that what is really humorous is the *content* of his parody. This becomes much clearer in his and Bricmont's book, whose central thesis runs approximately as follows: "French philosophers think there is no external world, but that's meaningless. French philosophy is nothing but fashionable nonsense." (Those who think I am caricaturing Sokal's argument need only look at the image of the Eiffel Tower on the cover.) In short, he attacks French philosophy not for the stale jargon and rampant careerist intrigues to which it has given rise in the United States: instead, he primarily wants to attack its *anti-realism*. But there are two problems with this polemic. In the first place, anti-realism is a perfectly legitimate philosophical position, with respectable defenders to be found as early as ancient Greece. While I too have grown increasingly unsympathetic to this aspect of contemporary philosophy, it is hardly "nonsense"; Sokal's targets are intelligent authors who should not be treated like an army of clowns. Second, and even more importantly for us today, Bruno Latour is not simply an anti-realist, as should be clear even from a few of the passages quoted by Sokal himself.

This brief discussion of the *Social Text* incident was meant as an important preliminary warning. Whatever else you may hear today or in the future, never believe anyone who tells you that Latour holds that "all reality is socially constructed". Whether this view can be wholly or partly ascribed to some of the other French thinkers on Sokal's list, I will leave it to you to decide. But there is no chance at all that it can hold good of Latour. Nor does this realization require some sort of subtle oblique approach to his works, for it is stated so obviously that it can only be overlooked by a lazy or prejudiced reading of his books.

The goal of what follows is twofold. First, I want to offer an introduction to Latour's work for the majority of this afternoon's audience not yet familiar with it; however, I do this more as a fan than as an expert. Second, I want to suggest that there is a whiff of the future about Latour's writings, and that his new model of reality ought to be vehemently championed by anyone desperate for new trends in contemporary continental thought. Accordingly, the tone of what follows will be half book report and half rebel yell. Following the presentation and the question period, you are invited to join me for another round of toasts at a dimly lit tavern at the corner of Racine and Montana.[23]

* * *

Bruno Latour is Professor of Sociology at the Centre de Sociologie de l'Innovation of the Ecole des Mines in Paris. When asked to describe the elusive discipline in which he works, he often refers to it as "science studies", as distinct from either the history or philosophy of science. An early protégé of Michel Serres, Latour is now a rising superstar in sociology and information studies, and has begun to receive serious notice from American philosophers as well (most of them working in the analytic tradition). Based on some of his scattered remarks and on his general appearance, I would estimate that he is not quite fifty years old. In any case, he is just beginning to enter his intellectual prime, and thus is sure to be a force for all of us to reckon with in the early part of the coming century. Indeed, given his strategic position between analytic and continental thought, between nature and technology, science and language, I am willing to predict that he might be the dominant philosophical figure on our landscape by around the year 2010.[24] And yet, it is only very recently that his name has begun to be heard in our vicinity. It is this discrepancy that led me to compose today's lecture.

Perhaps I should begin with a few words about Latour's general orientation. Latour is an engaging writer, pointedly hostile to established postmodern figures such as Baudrillard and Lyotard, although he does appear to have far more sympathy for a thinker such as Deleuze. He is filled with justifiable scorn for Heidegger's monotonous views on technology and the withdrawal of being, and displays perhaps even greater impatience with the works of Habermas. But although capable of brilliant polemical stabs, Latour's persona as an author is a notably patient and scholarly one. He is no anti-establishment flamethrower, but someone who believes strongly in the role of academic institutions and collective research programs, and in his lectures at Northwestern last spring gave the impression of being a friendly and approachable person.[25] Despite occasional self-references to his Gallic personality traits, his written work and public presentations have more of an informal American feel than the grave and opinionated talks that one is used to hearing from European intellectual stars. Best of all, he is certainly the wittiest philosopher working today in any tradition. Countless jokes and wry analogies litter his works, many of them reminiscent of the Deleuzian sense of humor.

The author of numerous articles in science studies, Latour is probably best known for his first five books, all of them available in English. 1979 saw the publication with co-author Steve

Woolgar of *Laboratory Life*, with a subtitle (*The Social Construction of Scientific Facts*) that may be responsible for many of the misunderstandings of his work in this country. In 1984 came the French version of the book that would appear in English four years later as *The Pasteurization of France*, an attempt to replace the "genius" interpretation of Pasteur with an analysis of all the various objects and forces that were mobilized in order for Pasteur's theories and vaccines to win acceptance; the second half of this book, *Irreductions*, offers an impressive systematic account of Latour's general position. His breakthrough work, *Science in Action*, was published in 1987; it is this particular volume that is widely regarded in the United States as his *magnum opus* up to now, although I would disagree with that assessment. The 140-page manifesto *We Have Never Been Modern*, issued in 1991, is the best concise summary of his thinking now available, and is the work I would recommend to those in this room as a good starting point. Latour's fifth book, the colorful and offbeat *Aramis*, is a literary exploration of the cancellation of the little-known Aramis system: a fully computerized replacement for the Paris subway, consisting of detachable individual cars that would move independently from any point in the city to any other without transfer. This last work rivals Francis Bacon's remarks on fire, Aristotle's definition of good luck, and Leibniz's "Drôle de Philosophie" fragment as the most entertaining philosophical text I have ever seen.

Today, I will focus almost exclusively on *We Have Never Been Modern*, which is not only a conveniently short work, but also the one that is probably most useful for framing Latour's specifically philosophical insights. It should be admitted at the outset that the result will be a somewhat unusual overview of Latour. Many of his fans do not share my strong interest in ontology, but are empirical researchers making use of his methods to describe specific technological artifacts. For example, colleagues of mine in Canada and England have used Latour's work to explore the ramifications of electronic currency. But in principle such work is applicable to anything that exists, since even flowers, rocks, and comets would have to count as actors. A case could be made that Latour is even more interesting as a reader of particular objects than as a theorist of objects in general, given his famous mobilization of Pasteur's microbes and Aramis's silicon-based actors. Be that as it may, it is ontology that interests me here. Those who want a taste of Latour's more concrete investigative work are urged to consult the additional works cited above.

The opening question of *We Have Never Been Modern* concerns the status of what Latour calls "hybrid" realities. The contemporary world, he observes, is filled with such hybrids. A newspaper article on the depletion of the ozone layer deals on the one hand with the scientific reality of this crisis: the hole is measurable, and apparently real. Or is it? The CEOs of some of the major chemical companies, under governmental pressure, are rushing to comply with the new regulations against chlorofluorocarbons. But suddenly a wrench is thrown into the works: meteorologists and climatologists propose that so-called global warming is actually the result of normal planetary fluctuations unrelated to human activity. All at once the ozone layer seems less like an objective physical fact than the locus of a power/knowledge struggle between competing interest groups. Is global warming something real, or something merely narrated? This is by no means a frivolous question, since profound policy decisions hinge on answering it. As Latour puts it: "The same article mixes together chemical reactions and political reactions. A single thread links the most esoteric sciences and the most sordid politics, the most distant sky and some factory in the Lyons suburbs.... none of these is commensurable, yet there they are, caught up in the same story."[26] As usual, Latour offers as many additional examples as he can, as much in the name of fun as of clarity. For instance: "On page twelve [of today's paper], the Pope, French bishops, Monsanto, the Fallopian tubes, and Texas fundamentalists gather in a strange [network] around a single contraceptive."[27]

At no place in any of these couplings is it possible to point to a term that is purely natural, since our access to the things-in-themselves is never direct, and since the gateway to any piece of knowledge is often the locus of a rhetorical competition or struggle. But by the same token there is no point in any of the connections that would be purely constructed or purely political: beyond all rhetoric, either we will all die of skin cancer or we will not. This has nothing to do with literary tropes or with the construction or death of the subject through the machinations of power. On the one hand there are Sokal and his cousins, insisting on the reality of the real and the secondary nature of social effects. On the other hand, there are the hipsters more clever than all objectivity, adopting a relentless critical stance that protects them from being duped by any naive notion of brute fact. It should be noted that Latour condemns both of these camps as equally misled.

Packed full with hybrids, the world is a Gordian knot. Latour's paradoxical claim about modernity is as follows. On the one hand, modernity produces monstrous couplings of various objects, conjunctions bizarre enough in our time that the word "surreal" has become part of our daily language. One day not so long ago we found *Hustler* publisher Larry Flynt and the Reverend Jerry Falwell linked up with the Constitution of the United States and some pornographic cartoons. Today, Prague and Budapest enter a machine that also contains a pair of stealth bombers from Missouri, plus some Orthodox monasteries, plus CNN, plus the ghost of the Ottoman Empire.[28] Shuffling objects into ever newer and stranger combinations, modernity creates monstrous unions between the most far-flung objects under the sun. But the second aspect of modernity, utterly opposed to this one, is its ceaseless *critical* stance. Modernity not only creates hybrids, but also assumes the intellectual task of purifying them, whether by bracketing all dogma and occult properties to arrive at a theory of nature in itself, or by turning a skeptical glance toward all scientific claims so as to view them as the surface effects of human political and linguistic convention.

In this way, the Gordian knot is cut. Either we defend nature as the key to reality, or hold that societal convention is the root of everything. Better yet, strategies can easily be devised that allow us to switch back and forth between these two positions whenever we please. American liberals have no problem shifting between the claims that homosexuality is genetic and that crime is environmental, while conservatives commit the equal hypocrisy of saying that poverty has always existed and always will even while demanding just enough social engineers to monitor swear words on the internet. In both cases we flip back and forth between two mutually exclusive explanatory theories, declaring every object and event to be either naturally occurrent or socially produced. Indeed, we oscillate between one and the other with increasing speed.

But Latour describes his philosophical aim as nothing less than the *retying* of the Gordian knot. The world is in each case a network of opinions, political institutions, chemicals, lakes, and written texts. The attempt to privilege one of these, to think the others out of existence, would be to repeat the attempted cleansing work of modernity. For the purposes of convenience, Latour describes three such types of cleansing. The first of these he terms "naturalization". Here, in a viewpoint closely related to that of common sense and openly defended by Sokal, it would be the physical objects that we would have to take as primary, with social factors as nothing but additional complications that arise after the fact. What is truly real according to this viewpoint is the objective existence or non-existence of the ozone hole, which only gets clouded by all the "irrational" power-struggles that cloud it over. But as Latour claims: "it becomes impossible to understand peptides without hooking them up with a scientific community, interests, practices— all impedimenta that bear very little resemblance to rules of method, theories, and neurons."[29]

The second method of purification, which might be termed "socialization", can be represented by Pierre Bourdieu. Here, "scientific truth [would be equivalent] to mere political interests, and technical efficiency to mere strategical maneuvers."[30] Yet we cannot talk about the fluctuations of social power without also talking about its relations to objects: "EDF and Renault take on a completely different look depending on whether they invest in fuel cells or the internal combustion engine; America before electricity and America after electricity are two different places...."[31] In short, the attempt to reduce all objects to political marionettes fails as quickly as naive realism.

The third form of purification, which Latour identifies as "deconstruction", can be roughly exemplified by Derrida. If we are not talking about external objective things or human power plays, "then [we] must be talking just about discourse, representation, language, texts, rhetoric."[32] Latour rejects this purification as much as the others: "When [Donald] MacKenzie examines the evolution of internal guidance systems [in missiles], he is talking about arrangements that can kill us all.... When I describe Pasteur's domestication of microbes, I am mobilizing nineteenth-century society, not just the semiotics of a great man's texts; when I describe the invention-discovery of brain peptides, I am really talking about the peptides themselves, not simply their representation in Professor Guillemin's laboratory."[33] In short, science deals neither with reality nor power nor rhetoric, but with all of these insofar as they belong to a network of animate and inanimate actors. As Latour concludes: "Rhetoric, textual strategies, writing, staging, semiotics— all these are really at stake, but in a new form that has a simultaneous impact on the nature of things and on the social context, while it is not reducible to one or the other."[34] While not mutually reducible, each of these zones is to some extent *translatable* into the others (cf. Michel Serres), a state of affairs described in the second half of the Pasteur-book as the "irreduction" of the sciences.

It should be clear by now that Latour is not saying that "reality is socially constructed", since this is only one of three attempted purifications that he regards as one-sided. Therefore, Richard Rorty completely misreads Latour when he states as follows: "We can say, with Foucault, that both human rights and homosexuality are recent human constructions, but only if we say, with Bruno Latour, that quarks are too."[35] Obviously, Rorty offers a reading of Latour that is heavily tinged with his own pragmatist crusade against nature-in-itself. But Rorty does this only so that human linguistic praxis can become the sole genuine reality in the cosmos, while Latour puts human action in its place no less than nature. Puzzled by the strange persistence of this misreading, I took the liberty on 8 November, 1998 of writing to Rorty in person to express my objections. That letter read in part: "Dear Professor Rorty.... Certainly, Latour does criticize the vision of the world according to which certain sorts of ideas or entities would be defined as natural, others as [only] human fabrications. But in the passage above, you seem to imply that he does this by defining *everything* as a construction. In fact, it strikes me that this is [precisely] the view that Latour criticizes...."[36] Somewhat to my surprise, Rorty responded one week later as follows: "Dear Professor Harman: Thanks for your letter. You are right that I should have left out [Bruno Latour] in that sentence. His view is much more complicated. What I wanted to say was that quarks are no more and no less social constructions than human rights, and that that shows that the real-vs.-socially constructed distinction can safely be neglected. Sincerely, Richard Rorty. November 16, 1998."[37]

But whereas Rorty "safely neglects" this distinction by means of a simple declaration that everything is social, Latour would view this step as just another modern purification movement.

Contra Rorty's privileging of human linguistic convention, what is primary is a network swarming with actors, agents, objects, each of them translating and displacing the forces of the others. In the end, access to my own private thoughts is every bit as mediated as access to the inner reality of a brick or a leaf. Reality is partly objective and partly perspectival. It is partly real, partly of a narrative character, and partly the effect of political displacements. Left in a thoroughly ambiguous situation, the zones of reality have a fate not unlike that of a stateless people: "The tiny networks we have unfolded are torn apart like the Kurds by the Iranians, the Iraqis and the Turks; once night has fallen, they slip across borders to get married, and they dream of a common homeland that would be carved out of the three countries which have divided them."[38]

The modern critical stance, he believes, thrives on an artificial separation between nature and culture, generally with the aim of reducing one to the other:

Because [they believe] in the total separation of humans and nonhumans, and because [they] simultaneously cancel out this separation.... the moderns [are] invincible. If you criticize them by saying that Nature is a world constructed by human hands, they will show you that it is transcendent, that science is a mere intermediary allowing access to Nature, and that they keep their hands off. If you tell them that we are free and that our destiny is in our own hands, they will tell you that Society is transcendent and its laws infinitely surpass us. If you object that they are duplicitous, they will show you that they never confuse the Laws of Nature with imprescribable human freedom. If you believe them and direct your attention elsewhere, they will take advantage of this to transfer thousands of objects from Nature into the social body while procuring for this body the solidity of natural things. Everything happens in the middle, everything happens by

way of mediation, translation and networks, but this space
does not exist [for the moderns], it has no place.[39]

Yet the supposed purification of the moderns has never actually
taken place. In spite of modernity's critical efforts, it has
continued to produce hybrids and networks on an even greater
scale than before, fusing rain forests and airlines and congres-
sional legislation, in precisely the same way that a South Pacific
tribe seems to foolishly mix ancestor worship with the causes of
hurricanes. Hence the title: *We Have Never Been Modern*. All this
time, there have really only been networks, hybrids, and
monsters. There was never any radical critical break with the
supposed tribal naivete that interpreted natural objects as signals
and omens for human affairs, and which likewise viewed human
songs and magic spells as potential forces of nature. What Latour
criticizes is the idea of modernity in any field as a radical critical
break with everything that came before; in his view, what has
really happened in all such cases is merely the redistribution of
actors along a network, and such networks have existed from
time immemorial.

What we find always and everywhere are simply networks of
actors. The actor is not quite an object and not quite a subject; or
rather, it can behave like both of these, depending on how we
view it. Following Serres, Latour makes use of the term "quasi-
object"[40] to refer to the precarious status of entities. On the one
hand they are contextualized by the objects with which they are
fused; on the other, they have retreated into their own dark inner
natures and are never fully measured by the networks in which
they are involved at any given moment. Parrots and ice-shelves
are not fully natural, since they are both absorbed and transformed by various networks of tourism, nature films, and
ecological depletion. They not only appear differently *to us* due to
all these factors, but their very reality is changed by them: parrots
grow fat by stealing catfood from Caribbean villages, or are

rendered extinct by bulldozers and acid rain. But by the same token, the internet is not something merely constructed. After all, the would-be human reformer cannot simply impose arbitrary renovations upon it, but must take its *reality* or *resistance* into account. Often the internet "crashes" with as much unpredictability as the arrival of a hailstorm; the fact that it is made of plastic and silicon is irrelevant. Once it is created, the internet simply exists: just like a snowflake, just like a jungle. These objects are not simple real objects in the naive sense, but *quasi-*objects.

Here we catch sight of Latour's tacit ontological thesis: every entity is both enslaved in a cultural/functional or perspectival system of meaning *and* has an undeniable reality to which human life is held hostage. In a little-known but fascinating essay on Whitehead,[41] Latour disclaims any theory of essence in favor of the strongly holistic network-ontology of Whitehead's *Process and Reality*. But insofar as he is forced to recognize that some aspect of every actor is *causa sui* and therefore withdrawn from the network, he moves toward a critique of extreme holism that lay beyond the means of Whitehead and his hot-blooded crusade against traditional substances. Within certain limits, the widely discredited "essentialism" must be reintroduced if an adequate theory of networks is ever to emerge. Elsewhere, I have argued that this is the implicit achievement of Heidegger's famous tool-analysis, but *We Have Never Been Modern* does the job more explicitly in some ways.

For all his apparent eagerness for an era of networks and actors in philosophy, Latour does not seem at all nervous or jumpy in pushing for the dawn of such an era. He seems to feel in a position to relax somewhat, largely because it is not primarily through his own efforts that a world of intellectual hybrids will emerge. He and his friends have no need to work like dogs or pull night-long study sessions in order to make this dream a reality. Rather, he believes that history itself is working to force philosophy to pay tribute to hybrids, quasi-objects, and networks. In a refreshing twist, the central date Latour chooses for this process is not 1968, but 1989. The death of the great ideologies, the collapse of a dual superpower conflict into regional vendettas, and the undeniable reemergence of objective physical reality in the environmental ruins of Eastern Europe and Valdez, all point to 1989 as a turning point. Various "cyborg" technologies will only increase this proliferation of hybrids. Eventually, everything reaches the point where if it is impossible to ignore the constructedness of quarks, it is equally impossible to ignore the naturalness of subway tunnels and giant electrical grids (this latter realization is the one that is usually missed). As Latour puts it:

> When the only thing at stake was the emergence of a few vacuum pumps, they could still be subsumed under two classes, that of natural laws and that of political representations; but when we find ourselves invaded by frozen embryos, expert systems, digital machines, sensor-equipped robots, hybrid corn, data banks, psychotropic drugs, whales outfitted with radar sounding devices, gene synthesizers, audience analyzers, and so on, when our daily newspapers display all these monsters on page after page, and when none of these chimeras can be properly on the object side or on the subject side, or even in between, something has to be done.... Where are we to classify the ozone hole story, or global warming or deforestation? Where are we to put these hybrids? Are they human? Human because they are our work. Are they natural? Natural because they are not our doing. Are they local or global? Both.[42]

I would like to cite one more Latourian criticism of the purifiers, since it is very clear and also gives an excellent taste of his often sardonic wit:

Social scientists have for long allowed themselves to denounce the belief system of ordinary people. They call this belief system 'naturalization'. Ordinary people imagine that the power of goods, the objectivity of money, the attraction of fashion, the beauty of art, come from some objective properties intrinsic to the nature of things. Fortunately, social scientists know better and they show that the arrow goes in fact in the other direction, from society to the objects. Gods, money, fashion and art offer only a surface for the projection of our social needs and interests.... To become a social scientist is to realize that the inner properties of objects do not count, that they are mere receptacles for human categories.[43]

But the opposite denunciation can occur just as easily:

Ordinary people, mere social actors, average citizens, believe that they are free and that they can modify their desires, their motives and their rational strategies at will.... But fortunately, social scientists are standing guard, and they denounce, and debunk and ridicule this naïve belief in the freedom of the human subject and society. This time they use the.... indisputable results of the sciences to show how [they] determine, inform, and mold the soft and pliable wills of the poor humans.... All the sciences (natural and social) are now mobilized to turn the humans into so many puppets manipulated by objective forces— which only the natural or social scientists happen to know.[44]

Latour believes that in ths way the moderns are always *seeing double*. Their usual recourse is to separate the world into "soft" and "hard" segments, "the 'soft' list.... gathering all those things social scientists happen to despise —religion, consumption, popular culture and politics— while the 'hard' list is made up of all the sciences they naively believe at the time— economics, genetics, biology, linguistics, or brain sciences."[45] One becomes comfortable with such a dualism, and feels little guilt about switching back and forth between them to an almost arbitrary degree. But never do the two cross over and fertilize one another.

Latour credits the Edinburgh school of science studies (beginning in the 1970's in the work of Barnes, Shapin, and Bloor) with initiating such a crossover:

> They used the critical repertoire that was reserved for the 'soft' parts of nature to debunk the 'harder' parts, the sciences themselves! In short, they wanted to do for science what Durkheim had done for religion, or Bourdieu for fashion and taste; [but] they innocently thought that the *social* sciences would remain unchanged, swallowing science as easily as religion or the arts.... [In this way,] the Edinburgh daredevils deprived the dualists —and indeed themselves, as they were soon to realize— of half of their resources. Society [now] had to produce everything arbitrarily including the cosmic order, biology, chemistry, and the laws of physics! The implausibility of this claim was so blatant for the 'hard' parts of nature that we suddenly realized how implausible it was for the 'soft' ones as well. Objects are not the shapeless receptacles of social categories— neither the 'hard' ones nor the 'soft' ones.... Society is neither that strong nor that weak; objects are neither that weak nor that strong. The double position of objects and society had to be entirely rethought.[46]

Much of this rethinking is done more effectively in Latour's specific case studies than anywhere else. Given his great respect for empirical research, it is difficult to grasp his methods fully without following him at work on a series of concrete problems. But in the limited time remaining to me today, I prefer to concentrate on Latour's potential contributions to an ontology of objects, which (as his work implies) is the best strategy for transforming present-day philosophy in a manner doing justice to all the hybrid artifacts now swarming about us. The best way to do this is to summarize briefly his objections to several rival contemporary theories, and then to imagine what a future philosophy guided by Latour's star might look like.

When Boyle and Hobbes dueled over whether the workings of an air pump should be interpreted in terms of nature or convention, the famous modern distinction between subject and object began to manifest itself. In Kant, the distinction becomes a full separation from which all of the more recent purifications have sprung. Guiltlessly criticizing the notion of Kant's "Copernican Revolution", Latour tosses another trademark grenade:

> This Kantian formulation is still visible today every time the human mind is credited with the capacity to impose forms arbitrarily on amorphous but real matter. To be sure, the Sun King around which objects revolve will be overturned in favor of many other pretenders— Society, epistemes, mental structures, cultural categories, intersubjectivity, language; but these palace revolutions will not alter the focal point, which I have called, for that reason, Subject/Society.[47]

It becomes the very mark of philosophical sophistication to heap scorn upon anything lying beyond the bounds of human accessibility. Eventually, only reactionary materialists are willing to defend the notion of discrete things-in-themselves. The mark of a real thinker is to remain confined to the human sphere, to see all reality as holistically interwoven. This is true of Heidegger, it is true of postmodernism, it is true in many respects even of Bergson, and it holds now for most analytic philosophers in the post-Quine mold.

But I would argue that these are precisely the two chief dogmas of contemporary philosophy: (a) anti-realism, and (b) holism. They represent perhaps the two greatest features of twentieth century philosophy, with its predominantly linguistic model of reality. But do they still have enough juice to sustain us for another hundred years? As I see it, the tacit answer suggested by Latour is "No". In the first place, it is necessary to take account of real objects once again, as Whitehead already sensed with his unabashed revival of pre-Kantian metaphysics. As mentioned earlier, it is not true that I have any more intimate access to language or consciousness or the conditions of speech-acts than I do to a pile of rocks. In both cases there is much that withdraws beyond my understanding; in both cases, there is much that truly resists my efforts to manipulate the world. The empirical fact that I happen to know my own secret thoughts better than the center of an uncut watermelon does not amount to a valid ontological privilege for thinking or language. The time has come to stop all of the chic wringing of hands about the inaccessibility of the referent, and to join Latour in endorsing a theory where propositions and psychoses interact with oilfields and dolphins. Obviously, more could be said about this theme, and I promise to say more next month at the "End of the Century" conference.[48]

As far as holism is concerned, it was a valuable gesture as long as the reigning dogma was that of positivism, stale substance-philosophies, or dogmatic realisms. But the notion of the whole preceding the part also tends to become a dogma in its own right, especially when bolstered by the language-centered models of reality that have dominated the latter part of this century in both analytic and continental thought. Holism is an idea once but no longer liberating. It is certainly true that objects determine one another by responding to each other, smashing into one another, and drawing each other into marriages, clubs, networks, and other unions. But it is equally true that they do not thereby vaporize into a systematic totality. The nails and bolts in a table do contribute to the table as a total unified entity, but do not cease for that reason to be bolts and nails. Rather, their continued participation in the table is renegotiated at each moment, and can easily be broken off due to the actions of workmen or vandals, or simply by internal structural flaws that cause the bolts and nails to collapse. The insights of holism should not be abused in order to slander the true independence of the entities that orbit freely through the cosmos, not dissolved into a single-world system as Heidegger would have it, but ensconced in monstrous hybrid relationships even while retaining their integrity, much as an organic eyeball and a metallic fist retain their independence in the body of a cyborg. As we are reminded by *Aramis*, the networks among things do not disintegrate the firewalls that define them as integral and quasi-inviolable regions.

Perhaps the best way to drive this point home, as well as to provoke further discussion later this afternoon, is simply to quote a few more of Latour's most interesting jabs. With any luck, this will also clarify a bit further how his model of the world differs from those of selected contemporaries. To begin with, there is the example of Habermas, who wishes to abandon any notion of language's referring to a referent so as to replace it with the mutual agreement of an ideal speech community. Latour remarks:

If anyone has ever picked the wrong enemy, it is surely this displaced twentieth-century Kantianism that attempts to widen the abyss between the objects known by the subject on the one hand, and communicational reason on the other.... The old consciousness at least had the merit of aiming at the object, and thus of recalling the artificial origin of the two.... poles. But Habermas wants to make [them] incommensurable, at the very moment when quasi-objects are multiplying [so much] that it appears impossible to find [either] a free speaking subject or a reified natural object. Kant was already unable to bring it off in the middle of the Industrial

Revolution; how could Habermas manage it after the sixth or seventh revolution?.... It is a bit too late to carry off the coup of the Copernican Revolution and make things revolve around intersubjectivity. Habermas and his disciples hold on to the modern project only by abstaining from all empirical enquiry— not a single case study in the five hundred pages of his masterwork.[49]

"Nonetheless," Latour says, "[Habermas] remains honest and respectable. Even in [his] caricature of the modern project we can still recognize the faded splendor of the nineteenth-century Enlightenment...."[50] A worse case in his eyes is posed by figures such as Baudrillard and Lyotard, whom he berates in the following terms: "I have not found words ugly enough to designate this intellectual movement— or rather, this intellectual immobility through which humans and non-humans are left to drift. I call it 'hyper-incommensurability....' 'You have nothing more to expect from us,' Baudrillard and Lyotard delight in saying. No indeed. But it is no more in their power to end history than it is to not be naive. They are simply stuck in the impasse of all avant-gardes that have no more troops behind them."[51]

With respect to the more semiotic versions of postmodernism, Latour again levels the charge that an artificial split is being made between subject, object, and discourse:

If [these three zones] are kept distinct, and if all three are separate from the work of hybridization, the image of the modern world they give is indeed terrifying: a nature and a technology that are absolutely sleek; a society made up of false consciousness, simulacra and illusions; a discourse consisting only in meaning effects detached from everything; and this whole world of appearances keeps afloat other disconnected elements of networks that can be combined haphazardly by collage from all places and all times.

Enough, indeed, to make one contemplate jumping off a cliff. Here is the cause of the postmoderns' flippant despair, one that has taken over from the angst of their predecessors, masters of the absurd. However, postmoderns would never have reached this degree of derision and dereliction had they not believed —to cap it all— that they had forgotten Being.[52]

And indeed, there may be no more enlightening moment in Latour's book than his irreverent slam of Heidegger, the worst offender at that modern crime of attempting to cleanse the hybrids by sequestering being and beings from one another. Latour notes that initially it may have looked as though Heidegger were on to something, with his "ontological difference" providing a safety zone far from all idealism and all linguistic turns. Here at last was a great philosopher willing to treat the hybrid *Zwischen* ("between") with the respect it deserves (as I have also argued in my recently defended dissertation *Tool-Being*). "Quasi-objects do not belong to Nature, or to Society, or to the subject; they do not belong to language, either. By deconstructing metaphysics [a.k.a. the illegitimate purifying process of modernity], Martin Heidegger designates the central point where everything holds together, remote from subjects and objects alike."[53]

So far, so good. The problem arises when Heidegger attempts a purifying movement of his own with the claim that being itself can never reside in ordinary beings. Here, the reader can already sense the approach of a final Latourian rampage against twentieth century philosophy, and it is not long in coming. Latour deftly uses one of Heidegger's own parables against him, recalling the townspeople who were surprised at the sight of Heraclitus warming himself at a baker's oven. In response to their surprise Heraclitus famously replied: "Here too the gods are present." And this is where Latour takes off the gloves:

But Heidegger is taken in as much as these naive visitors, since he and his epigones do not expect to find Being except along the Black Forest Holzwege. Being cannot reside in ordinary beings. Everywhere, there is desert. The gods cannot reside in technology— that pure Enframing of being, that ineluctable fate, that supreme danger. They are not to be sought in science, either, since science has no other essence but that of technology. [The gods] are absent from politics, sociology, psychology, anthropology, history— which is the history of Being, and counts its epochs in millennia. The gods cannot reside in economics— that pure calculation forever mired in beings and worry. They are not to be found in philosophy, either, or in ontology, both of which lost sight of their destiny 2,500 years ago. Thus Heidegger treats the modern world as the visitors treat Heraclitus: with contempt.[54]

And then, in one of those passages that I would kill to have written myself:

And yet— 'here too the gods are present': in a hydroelectric plant on the Rhine, in subatomic particles, in Adidas shoes as well as in the old wooden clogs hollowed out by hand, in agribusiness as well as in timeworn landscapes, in shopkeepers' calculations as well as in Hölderlin's heartrending verse.[55]

I now conclude this brief survey of the work of Bruno Latour, arguably the freshest voice in contemporary French philosophy. As I have tried to share with you today, there are several negative and positive virtues that can be found even in the briefest outline of this work. Negatively, he rejects the familiar strict separations between subject and object, nature and culture, being and beings. The modern movement of purification ruins the character of quasi-objects, which are shattered by such rude handling. Every form of linguistic turn, every human-centered approach to philosophy must be rejected, but without falling back into a naive realism of the type championed by Sokal and others. The world is a network of actors, and there is no need to segregate these actors into natural and socially produced: the real, Latour says, is simply whatever *resists* various trials of strength.

Positively, Latour paints a world in which objects couple and uncouple their forces while still existing with a certain degree of genuine independence. The interaction of nations, rivers, armies, scientific discoveries, geniuses, and iron ore should be studied in the same way that we analyze gas lines or sewage pipes. The new species of thinker called for is half-philosopher and half-engineer, as the elusive unions of actors are painstakingly disassembled for our view: philosophy as *reverse engineering*. Instead of returning to a metaphysics that tries to transcend the contaminating power of entities, philosophy becomes an "infra-physics".[56]

In this way, beyond the interplay of signifiers and images, a sense of undeniable reality begins to reappear. And furthermore, the still fashionable privileging of the system over its discrete parts begins to recede: in Latour's networks, the actors do retain independent properties that can resist or even subvert the entire system. In this way, he offers an alternative to anti-realism and an alternative to holism, which is enough to establish him as the most innovative philosophical writer working today. Above all, he is someone who allows for the return of concrete objects to philosophy, after their long exile decreed by those who were too clever to talk about paper, donkeys, and marbles, and therefore allowed themselves to speak only of the aloof and alienated cogito-linguistic structures that make all such objects possible.

Admittedly, this was not entirely the fault of those clever people, since the intellectual resources for a theory of objects still remain somewhat primitive. What *is* the fault of such people, however, is their arrogant assumption that things will always remain this way. As mentioned on another occasion, we should all hope to reach our intellectual primes in a world where it is once again possible to give philosophical lectures not just on "wood" as a literary figure in the works of Joyce or Mallarmé, but heartfelt lectures on *wood itself*: a systematic ontology of maple, oak, and cedar. Let's dream of a conference in the year 2020, to be held perhaps in this very building, that would openly wrestle with the reality of objects such as sailboats, grapefruit, wax, and platinum. For here too, the gods are present.

6. Object-Oriented Philosophy (1999)

This lecture was given on the soon to be ominous date of 11 September, 1999, at a conference at Brunel University in Uxbridge, England, close to London's Heathrow Airport. Bruno Latour was present for the lecture, just one day after I had spoken with him for the first time. The title of this lecture was the first occurrence of the phrase "object-oriented philosophy" in my writings.

As twentieth century philosophy enters its final months, there have been fewer retrospective surveys of its past one hundred years than might have been expected. Whether this is due to widespread disorientation or the understandable wish to avoid melodrama is anyone's guess. But at least one historical model of philosophy is being aired on a regular basis. This is the view that the great philosophical achievement of our century lies in its "linguistic turn". The philosophy of language is praised for having replaced an obsolete "philosophy of consciousness." Instead of an aloof human subject that merely observes the world while managing to keep its fingers clean, the human being now appears as a less autonomous figure, unable to escape fully from a network of linguistic significations and historical projections.

One of the usual selling points of this model is that it is equipped to offer praise to *both* of the rival strands of analytic and Continental philosophy. One side can be proud of the contributions to the linguistic turn made by Frege and Davidson, the other side proud for similar reasons of Saussure and Derrida. The two churches, it is said, are closer to reunification than we think. In retrospect, the great philosophical mission of the century will have been to replace the *theoretical* model of knowledge with a *hermeneutic* model. All naive commitment to absolute knowledge will have ended, and with it all naive belief in a world-in-itself that might be neutrally observed. Interpretation replaces vision.

But this version of twentieth century philosophy contains a notable flaw. The ostensibly revolutionary transition from consciousness to language still leaves humans in absolute command at the center of philosophy. All that happens is that the lucid, squeaky-clean ego of phenomenology is replaced by a more troubled figure: a drifter determined by his context, unable fully to transcend the structures of his environment. In both cases the inanimate world is left by the wayside, treated as little better than dust or rubble. When rocks collide with wood, when fire melts glass, when cosmic rays cause protons to disintegrate, we are asked to leave all of this to the physicists alone. Philosophy has gradually renounced its claim to have anything to do with the world itself. Fixated on the perilous leap between subject and object, it tells us nothing about the chasm that separates tree from root or ligament from bone. Forfeiting all comment on the realm of objects, it sets itself up as master of a single gap between self and world, where it holds court with a never-ending sequence of paradoxes, accusations, counter-charges, partisan gangs, excommunications, and alleged renaissances.

But beneath this ceaseless argument, reality is churning. Even as the philosophy of language and its supposedly reactionary opponents both declare victory, the arena of the world is packed with diverse objects, their forces unleashed and mostly unloved. Red billiard ball smacks green billiard ball. Snowflakes glitter in the light that cruelly annihilates them, while damaged submarines rust along the ocean floor. As flour emerges from mills and blocks of limestone are compressed by earthquakes, gigantic mushrooms spread in the Michigan forest. While human philosophers bludgeon each other over the very possibility of "access" to the world, sharks bludgeon tuna fish and icebergs smash into coastlines.

All of these entities roam across the cosmos, inflicting blessings and punishments on everything they touch, perishing without a trace or spreading their powers further, as if a million animals had broken free from a zoo in some Tibetan cosmology. Will philosophy remain satisfied with not addressing any of these objects by name, so as to confine itself to a "more general" discussion of the condition of the condition of the condition of possibility of ever referring to them? Will philosophy continue to lump together monkeys, tornadoes, diamonds, and oil under the single heading of that-which-lies-outside? Or is there some possibility of an object-oriented philosophy, a sort of alchemy for describing the transformations of one entity into another, for outlining the ways in which they seduce or destroy humans and non-humans alike? This lecture endorses the latter option.

Best of all, there is no need to start from scratch. Against the wide consensus that the virtue of twentieth century philosophy lies in its linguistic turn, I would argue that a more important but more concealed trend of the past one hundred years lies in the halting initial steps that have been taken toward a general theory of objects, steps taken until recently only in a sort of raw, pre-Socratic way. Since those relevant authors who are still alive and flourishing can speak for themselves, I will confine myself here to a pair of deceased thinkers. In my view the two most important systematic philosophers of the century now ending are Martin Heidegger and Alfred North Whitehead: one of them badly misread, the other badly underread. In the works of both, despite a serious shared mistake, there begins to reappear in philosophy a thirst for knowledge concerning the fate of specific objects. My goal today is to show why this is happening, and to sketch briefly several of the problems, both old and new, that are thereby unlocked in the heart of the things themselves.

I will begin with Heidegger, generally the better known of the two figures just mentioned. It is my contention that the key to the entire Heideggerian philosophy lies in the famous tool-analysis

95

of *Being and Time*. Although this has apparently been said dozens of times already, the commentators who state it are inevitably misreading Heidegger's tool as if it were related to pragmatism, or exemplified an early version of his later meditation on technology. My own view, admittedly an unorthodox one, is that the tool-analysis sketches nothing less than a general object-oriented philosophy, one that is by no means free of metaphysical elements. It also seems to me that this tool-analysis still represents the high-water mark of recent philosophy. Not only has it not been surpassed, it has not even been properly exploited.

The tool-analysis itself can be summarized rather easily. Heidegger observes that the primary reality of entities is not their sheer existence as pieces of wood or metal or atoms. The wood in a primitive sword and that in a modern windmill occupy utterly different niches of reality, unleash completely different forces in the world. A bridge is not a mere conglomerate of bolts and trestles, but a total geographic force to reckon with: a unitary bridge-effect. But even this unified bridge-machine is far from an absolute, obvious unit. It too has a vastly different reality depending on whether I cross it on the way to a romantic liaison or as a prisoner underway to execution. In one case it is equipment for rapture, in the other a means toward damnation and misery.

Things are so intimately related to their purposes, and these to still further purposes, that in Heidegger's view it is impossible to speak in a strict sense of "an" equipment. Instead of being a solid object that enters into relation only by accident, an entity in its reality is determined by the shifting, capricious storm of references and assignments in which it is enveloped. The displacement of the tiniest grain of dust on Mars alters the reality of the system of objects, however slightly. To introduce Heidegger's own terminology, entities are not primarily present-at-hand (*vorhanden*), but ready-to-hand (*zuhanden*).

When equipment is most equipment, it is concealed from view as something silently relied upon. As I invest all of my conscious

energy in reading aloud the words on this paper, I depend incon-
spicuously upon a vast tribe of additional objects taken for
granted: whether it be the artificial light in this room, breathable
air, the structural skeleton of this building, the security forces of
Brunel University who prevent hooligans from entering, or even
my own bodily organs. All of these objects remain loyal for the
moment, performing a subterranean function with which I have
no need to trouble myself, unless catastrophe strikes and one of
them fails. For Heidegger, it is generally when equipment is
lacking in some way that it emerges from its shadowy underground of pure competence and reveals its contours to view. If
the city suddenly loses electrical power, if I should begin to
cough uncontrollably, I am rudely reminded of entities previously taken for granted. There is an upsurge of bulky presence
into my environment.

Everywhere, the world is divided into these two opposed
poles: tool and broken tool, invisible action and obtrusive
presence. Equipment is a Janus-head. This does not hold true
only for those relatively rare cases in which objects literally
"break". For Heidegger, the same reversal is found wherever
objects are perceived, revealed by theoretical investigation, or
simply located in a specific region of space. In each of these
cases, he says, the veiled reality of equipment-in-action is torn
loose from the all-devouring system of the world, and set on
display "as" what it is.

But the very term "tool" can be seriously misleading. For it
has led most interpreters to suppose that Heidegger is talking
about one limited *kind* of object among others: as if the analysis
held good only of hammers, drills, keys, and windows, and not
for other objects with a less utilitarian status. But in fact
equipment in Heidegger's sense is global; beings are tool-beings.
To refer to an object as a "tool-being" is not to say that it is
brutally exploited as means to an end, but only that it is torn
apart by the universal duel between the silent execution of an

object's reality and the glistening aura of its tangible surface. In short, the tool isn't "used"; it *is*. What saves the bridge from being a mere pile of iron and asphalt is not the fact that people find it convenient, but the fact that any pile of anything exerts some sort of reality in the cosmos, altering the landscape of being in some distinct way. If this reality happens to be useful for people, so much the better. But natural mountain passes and other obstacles have no less equipmentality than an artificial tunnel. *Zuhandenheit* is an ontological term.

Withdrawing into its cryptic efficacy, equipment necessarily remains to a large degree a mystery, hidden from the crusading theorist and the tinkering civil engineer to an equal degree. Tool-being cannot be clarified by human praxis, which always relies upon it or is embedded in it. The key to the tool-analysis is not that it undermines the notion of solid Newtonian blocks with a people-centered analysis of plans and projections. The key is that it shows us that descriptions of the object as solid material *and* descriptions of it as functionally useful are derivative. More fundamental than both of these is the inscrutable empire of equipment from which all individual beings emerge. This empire is loaded with surprises.

There has been speculation as to whether the history of philosophy has a cyclical character, such that recent philosophy would mark a repetition of the full sequence of ideas found in ancient philosophy. Whether this claim can be sustained or not, there is sufficient reason to compare Heidegger to Parmenides, with his famous invocation that "being is, and non-being is not". Like this early Greek thinker whom he so admires, Heidegger too seems locked into repeating an awesomely simple dualism without being able to develop it more concretely: namely, the difference between the executant reality of an object and its encountered surface. Given more time, it could easily be shown that on every concrete topic Heidegger has nothing more to offer us than the famous ambiguous drama of concealing and revealing. Heidegger is the contemporary Parmenides.

To be at least somewhat specific, it could be shown that his celebrated theory of time has nothing to do with time at all. This word is simply one of his many literary figures for naming the single repetitive duality found throughout his works. All that emerges from his "temporal" analysis of a hammer is that the hammer must be regarded both as the execution of a real effect (a.k.a. "past") and as a discrete reality determined by its significance for a human involved in a specific projection of the world (a.k.a. "future"). The ambiguous co-existence of these two moments gives us Heidegger's "present". Voilà! There you have it: the supposed Heideggerian theory of time, which would hold good even if a sorcerer were able to freeze time forever in its tracks. The same monotonous analysis occurs when Heidegger claims to be telling us about technology, human moods, artworks, animal organisms, or indeed *any* supposed concrete topic in his fifty-six volumes of 17,000 pages (published so far). While this is not widely recognized, it is one of the main sources of the unpleasant aftertaste familiar to anyone who has ever read Heidegger for several consecutive hours.

To return to the main theme, there is a ubiquitous opposition in Heidegger's thought between two modes of being: those known as "ready-to-hand" and "present-at-hand". The easy step would be to read this opposition in a traditional way, as if the first belonged to the sphere of the "object" and the second to that of the "subject". The tool would seem equivalent to the brute force of inanimate causation, the "broken" tool to human perception or the human capacity to transcend the immediate environment, stepping beyond and reflecting critically on the environment "as" what it is. But we must immediately rid ourselves of this framework by making several remarks that would cause Heidegger himself to become either furious or coldly dismissive. Here is one of them: the dualism between tool and broken tool actually has no need of human beings, and would hold perfectly well of a world filled with inanimate entities alone. Let's say that a person is confronted with the proverbial pair of billiard balls. We have already seen that for Heidegger, these balls are not reducible to that which the player *encounters* of them. Withdrawn into the performance of their deepest reality, they can only be partly objectified or unveiled by an observer. This is fine. The problem lies in assuming that the two balls in collision to do not also objectify each other, as if humans faced a world of still unperceived depths but inanimate objects exhausted one another's reality upon the slightest contact. Ball Number One may be shiny and hot to the touch. Ball Number Two will of course be utterly insensitive to these properties. And yet the shininess is somehow present for the beam of light that skids off the surface of the shiny ball and is deflected off into the galaxy. And the heat of the ball is overwhelming for the loose speck of ice that dissolves instantly upon touching it. In other words, even inanimate objects are caught up in something like a "hermeneutic circle". No object ever sucks all the juice out of another object. Is there any difference, then, between human perception and sheer physical causation? Of course: but Heidegger's ontology is not the place to find it. His recurrent duality between real thing and the way it is encountered by other things turns out to be far more encompassing than he would like, given his untenable belief that he begins with an account of human Dasein alone.

So much for Heidegger. Since the time allotted for this lecture is running out, it is unavoidable that Whitehead will receive only cursory treatment. But by way of compensation, it may be noted that the foregoing interpretation of Heidegger is a largely Whiteheadian one. Whereas Heidegger does intend to confine his tool-analysis to the sphere of human existence and its perils, and whereas I have had to do violence to Heidegger's intentions in order to apply it to objects in general, Whitehead openly embraces inanimate reality. As the latest advocate of a monadic theory of the cosmos, he is never shy about utilizing words such as "thought" or "feeling" to refer to the inner life of a stick or piece of hair.

Otherwise, the same dualism found in Heidegger is present in Whitehead as well. Where Heidegger refers to *Vorhandenes* as the thing insofar as it is objectified, Whitehead makes use of his "eternal object", a more Platonized version of a similar concept. There are enough subtle differences between the two pairs of terms that someone might object to any direct identification of them. Given lack of time to argue the point, I will merely assert it, while citing as peripheral evidence an even more powerful connection between these two seldom-linked ontologists. I refer to their obvious tendency always to grant philosophical primacy to the network of entities rather than to isolated individuals. When Heidegger insists that there is ultimately no such thing as "an" equipment, it is inevitable that we hear echoes of Whitehead's doctrine of the *single* concrescence in terms of which all actual entities are thoroughly defined. In both cases, nothing about the object is held in reserve from the full system of objects. In each moment, every entity is exhaustively deployed.

The result of this doctrine, or perhaps the cause of it, is the near-paranoia of both Whitehead and Heidegger concerning the possibility of enduring classical substances. The solemn Heidegger degrades the notion of durable material while the more good-natured Whitehead scoffs just as visibly at any idea of substances capable of undergoing adventures in space and time. For each of these figures, the tiniest incident or most whimsical human action has the surprising power to change the entire universe; the pettiest event alters the total relational system that embraces all objects. Note Whitehead's dismissive attitude, rare among the religious, of the very question concerning the immortality of the soul. Why worry about this, after all, when in a strict sense the soul does not even endure from one moment to the next? Despite his claim to strike a temperate balance between individuals and the whole, there is an extremely weak sense of the individual in his work. The object becomes merely a slang term for some region of the total concrescence. It is deprived of anything that would not be expressed in the world-system *hic et nunc*: stripped of all armor, all firewalls, all privacy. In short, it is vaporized into an infinitely interconnected empire.

A specter haunts this twentieth century doctrine: the specter of classical theories of substance. For Aristotle as for Leibniz, it is possible at least in principle to sift through the world and divide the substances from the non-substances. The title *substantia* is a reward handed out to certain entities but denied to many more. This occurs in most entertaining form in Leibniz's sometimes vitriolic correspondence with Arnauld. Leibniz asks us to imagine two diamonds: one belonging to the Grand Duke, the other to the Great Mogul. We can speak of these diamonds as a pair, but this pair is nothing more than "a thing of reason". Bringing the two diamonds closer together will not convert them into a single substance, not even if they were glued together. For if two diamonds glued together were a substance, Leibniz says, then a flock of birds would be a substance, and so would a circle of men holding hands. He apparently considers this observation to be a proof by *reductio ad absurdum*. But we need only recall that for Heidegger and Whitehead, a circle of men holding hands would be every bit as real a unity as the hardest diamond or the purest soul. For them, temporal endurance is never a valid criterion for reality.

It is in their shared tendency to reduce the world to nothing but a shifting system of relations that the common mistake of these twentieth-century thinkers must be located. A brief thought experiment will show some of the difficulties entailed by their position. Let's say that a chunk of plutonium is abandoned in the desert, compressing the sand on which it sits, deflecting sunlight into distant space, with no living creature anywhere in the vicinity. This artificial metal is ready-to-hand in the broadest Heideggerian sense. It is not just a pile of atoms that happens to have uses afterwards, but is primarily a specific agent that accomplishes certain deeds in the world while not accomplishing numerous others. But while the sand and dead weeds now surrounding the plutonium fail to sound the depths of its lethal radioactive quality, any living creatures that *were* present would be killed in minutes. In short, there is an additional reality in this strange artificial material that is in no way exhausted by the unions and associations in which it currently happens to be entangled. This reality is unexpressed, and will always remain so.

The usual easy way out of this predicament is the appeal to "potentiality" to explain the status of the radioactivity prior to the arrival of any animals. It will be said that the plutonium is not "actually" lethal, but potentially so given the right circumstances. What is weak about this approach (and given its illustrious classical pedigree, I realize that I will appear to be on thin ice) is that the theme of potential allows us a sneaky way to evade the difficult question of what the *actuality* of the lethal quality is. To speak of a quality in terms of its potential is already to speak of it from the outside, to objectify it rather than to clarify its ontological status. What is the actuality of the "lethal" here? Or in other words, just what is it that is "potentially" lethal in this case? Atoms? Or something far more strange?

1. Obviously, it cannot be the metal in its current state of relations that is potentially deadly, i.e. in its relations with sand and light and dead weeds. For by definition this system of relations is no longer itself once we add new elements to it. To use Whitehead's terms, "plutonium and sunlight" is not the same concrescence as "plutonium and sunlight and dying cat".

2. The commonsense belief would be that the actuality here is the physical mass of plutonium atoms, an enduring substrate

7. The Revival of Metaphysics in Continental Philosophy (2002)

In 2000 I left DePaul for a new job at the American University in Cairo, Egypt. One of the best features of this position has been the easy travel opportunities afforded by Cairo's location. On 30 April, 2002 I gave the following lecture at the American University of Beirut (which despite its name has no connection with the American University in Cairo), on my second visit to beautiful Lebanon. Unsure at the time of my future in Cairo, I was in Beirut as a finalist for a position there. One of the interesting features of this leture is the occurrence of the phrase "vicarious cause". This was also my first time speaking to an audience made up primarily of analytic philosophers, which helps provide context to my remarks on the differences between analytic and continental philosophy. The publication of Tool-Being *was still four months away; I had no publications to my name other than sports articles and a single translation of a book from German to English.*

The revival of metaphysics in continental philosophy is not yet underway. This paper is not a report, but in one sense a wish list and in another sense a possible "how to" manual. For the purposes of this lecture, the phrase "continental philosophy" refers to all present-day philosophy that takes its primary orientation from the phenomenological movement, whether in a positive or negative spirit. My central target will be Martin Heidegger and his various French descendants, who still very much dominate the subfield of continental philosophy, always ruled by an anti-metaphysical spirit. As a rule, continental philosophers take pride in not being duped by any notion of a real world distinct from the play of appearances. They imagine themselves to have made a radical break with traditional philosophy, which they regard as biased in favor of material things or independent essences: "essentialism" serves as an alternative pejorative term for "metaphysics". Prior to any individual things there is a context, a play of mutually differentiating signifiers. There is no essence anywhere; reality is radically contextual and radically plural. I speak here of the post-Heideggerian school. For more traditional phenomenologists there is of course still an essence to things, but it is always an essence that *appears*, so that to speak of a hidden essence would be a failure of method. As you may already have noted, views of this kind are by no means confined to continental philosophy. But it is here that they are least threatened by dissent. I cannot think of a single continental philosopher who has made a serious effort to defend the credentials of an independent reality beyond appearance, of a substance beyond every series of qualities, of a world-in-itself in which the human subject plays just one limited part.[57] Indeed, these claims evoke the sort of conservatism that continental philosophy believes it was born to destroy. Among continental philosophers, "metaphysician" remains as brutal an insult as it is among many working scientists. In this respect, it shares something in common with mainstream Anglo-American philosophy of language.

One thing it does *not* share in common with this other tradition is its attitude toward the history of philosophy. What continental philosophers hate most about analytic philosophers, what makes their blood boil late at night, is the practice of treating the history of philosophy in terms of "arguments". To take just one example: Russell's book on Leibniz is despised not because Russell's arguments are held to be *wrong*, but because it is regarded as an act of intellectual butchery to reduce him to arguments at all. What is important for the continentals is not a set of arguments made by Leibniz about substance, but rather something called "Leibniz's project", a total worldview that is not supposed to be cut up easily into discrete tiny pieces. Let this single example suffice. Already, the different attitudes of these two schools are clear. Analytic philosophy has tended to view philosophy as a matter of rigor or acuity, continental philosophy as a matter of genius. The great genre of analytic philosophy is the twenty-page journal article on a specific theme; in continental philosophy, journal articles play no important role whatsoever, with rare exceptions. Professor A thinks that Professor C is a fuzzy romantic with nothing clear to say; Professor C thinks that Professor A is a bloodless technician with no feel for the nuances of intellectual history. If the analytics can sometimes be accused of reducing past figures to the narrow strictures of contemporary frontline debates, the continentals are often guilty of feeling intimidated by their own heroes, never daring to criticize them at all, reducing much of its scholarship to the level of book reports. If analytic philosophy's openness to argument gives it a reputation for sometimes vicious oral debate, continental philosophy's contempt for mere argument has made it cliquish and impenetrable to newcomers, including those with something fresh and genuine to offer.

The point of these introductory remarks is to zero in on several related vices of contemporary continental philosophy, whether these be shared with other schools or not. First, there is the bias that I will call "the philosophy of access". Instead of discussing reality itself, we must first perform a series of sophisticated critical and self-reflexive maneuvers so as to ensure that we are only talking about objects as they manifest themselves to us, not about objects in their own inner life. In continental philosophy this has reached the point of tacit dogma, challenged by no one.

Second, there is the related bias that I will call "the philosophy of contexts or networks". The notion of independent substance or essence is supposedly naive. What comes first is the totality of meanings or objects in their reciprocal relations; any individual part of this network is nothing but an abstraction broken away from the system as a whole. This too is an unspoken dogma of continental philosophy: unspoken in the sense that no alternatives are ever proposed.

Finally, there is the bias that figures in the history of philosophy must always be read holistically, not used as a source for discrete ideas or arguments. There are some surprises connected with this point. For the supreme irony is that despite the great reverence of continental philosophers for major historical figures, they do not view them as serious competitors at all. The history of philosophy, in the continental view, is made up of a series of radical epistemological breaks (dated variously as beginning with Plato, Kant, Heidegger, or Derrida). When someone of the Heideggerian school writes about Aristotle or Hegel, this is usually done only to catalog a fateful, dark historical turn that permanently conditions everything coming afterward. It is done in the most somber possible tones. As a result, it would be unthinkable for continental philosophers to state a research problem and then to claim, for instance, that Husserl had it partly right, but St. Thomas Aquinas or Ibn Sina was closer to the mark on another aspect of the problem. If the strength of continental philosophy's historical awareness is its ability to preserve great past thinkers against the trivial claims of passing fashion, the weakness is equally obvious: continental philosophy is simply unable to treat past philosophers as contemporaries. Past philosophers do not join us in confronting a shared world against which all of us measure our insights, but swim in a historically conditioned ether that refers only to itself. It would make no sense to engage in debate with, say, Nicholas of Cusa on some specific issue without first situating this issue in his entire written corpus, mastering Latin, and so forth. Any past philosophy is too self-enclosed to serve as a possible model of the world, and too seamless to be harvested for specific insights.

The goal of this paper is to show how continental philosophy can and must abandon these biases. The radical anti-metaphysical stance of the continentals has become stale and fruitless, and its approach to the history of philosophy has stripped that history of its challenge. In what follows, I will argue that continental philosophy needs a total overhaul in the name of realism and essentialism, though perhaps not in the usual sense of these terms. Best of all, this overhaul is not a command coming from the outside, but is actually required by the central philosophical insight of Heidegger, who is the very pillar of continental philosophy. For all of Heidegger's famous polemics against metaphysics, he actually turns out to be a kind of guerilla metaphysician, whatever his intentions to the contrary.

In looking at Heidegger, it makes sense to focus on the tool-analysis of *Being and Time,* which is certainly his most popular argument and probably the one most central to his work. The basic point of the analysis seems to be simple. For the most part human beings do not encounter objects as blocks of physical matter or as subjects of theoretical inquiry. Prior to this we are immersed in a system of equipment, taking objects for granted while rarely noticing them at all. At this very moment we are all making use of numerous items of equipment. The ground beneath our feet gives stability to our movements, although we rarely remember this. The chemical composition of the air allows us to breathe easily and unreflectively. Our lungs and kidneys are silently at work keeping us alive, almost always unnoticed. A building like this one requires thousands of pieces of interconnected boards, tubes, and wires, each of them invisibly performing some vital function without our ever considering it. The objects of our explicit consciousness seem to form a thin and volatile film atop a heavy layer of equipment that is usually not seen, but only relied upon: the usual way of being of objects is *reliability.* Note that although Heidegger speaks of "tools", and although most of his examples are such things as hammers and railway platforms, the tool-analysis actually holds good for anything. All objects are encountered more often as tacit components of our world than as blatant objects of awareness. This is just as true of people, numbers, and religious edifices as of shovels and drills. Heidegger's tool-analysis is actually a universal theory of entities, although this point is still missed by the majority of his commentators.

The other famous part of Heidegger's analysis is the negative part: the discussion of broken tools. On the whole, we tend to notice objects only when they somehow malfunction. The light bulb is ignored until it burns out; the broken-down bus is noticed more than the one that arrives on time. Earthquakes and house fires make us appreciate former comforts that have now been destroyed. Heidegger actually treats all conscious awareness as a variant of broken equipment. To notice something openly, to perceive it or think about it, requires that we somehow tear ourselves away from part of the world and rise above it. Just as the word "tool" refers universally to all objects in their silent performance of an invisible function, so does "broken tool" refer to anything in its manifest visibility. The analysis of tools and broken tools has an unlimited scope, covering all entities, not just narrowly "useful" ones. The world is split into two parts: the tool in action and the tool in disrepair. Somewhat controversially, I would argue that if this analysis is followed patiently it can be shown to contain the entire content of Heidegger's philosophy, which is much simpler and much clearer than is usually believed. The question of being, the analysis of time, the later cluster of mystical German terms such as *Ereignis* and *das Geviert*, all turn out to be no more than sophisticated variants of the analysis of the hammer and its breakdown. Since Heidegger is not the primary theme of this paper, I will leave it at that.

The usual reading of the tool-analysis runs somewhat as follows. Theory must be grounded in practice, since all visibility emerges from a kind of pragmatic background. This background is made up of unthematic social practices and linguistic usages, so that social reality or language conditions all theory. The tool-analysis must also be staunchly anti-realist, since it seems to claim that things have no independent objective reality, but emerge only from a total system of human meanings. Finally, the tool-analysis represents an extreme form of holism, since Heidegger says the entire network of equipment is what is real, with each individual object being no more than an abstraction from this whole. "Strictly speaking", says Heidegger, "there is no such thing as *an* equipment." In the first chapter of my forth-coming book, I claim that all these assumptions are wrong. And although I believe that they distort our interpretation of Heidegger, what is far worse is that they have trapped conti-nental philosophy in a dead end. Most continental fans of Heidegger exult that he seems to subordinate the independent existence of objects to the total system of human usage. Indeed, it may be the case that he intended to do this; there is evidence both for and against. But in a way this is irrelevant, since I am more interested in the tool-analysis than in Heidegger himself, and the force of his analysis takes us in a different direction from the one he may have expected.

As already mentioned, the tool-analysis is usually read as arguing that praxis comes before theory, and also before any scientifically objective concept of things. But this seems clearly false. At this moment I am relying on countless items of equipment including floor, sunlight, and bodily organs. These tend to be invisible to me unless they malfunction. But the point is not that I am "using" them: the point is that I can only use them because they are real, because they are capable of inflicting some sort of blow on reality. The point is not just that my conscious awareness of the sun is grounded in my earlier practical use of it. The point is that both conscious and unconscious relations to the sun are grounded in the reality of the sun itself. The tool isn't "used"; it *is*. The tool-being of the sun is not its usefulness, but rather its silent performance of its own reality prior to any theoretical *or* practical contact we might have with it.

This can be phrased a bit differently. Heidegger refers to our conscious awareness of objects as a kind of "as-structure". To encounter a thing is to encounter it "as" such and such— as having certain explicit qualities. When the subway system breaks, or when we decide to study it in a research project, we become aware of many of its properties that were previously hidden. To become explicitly aware of an object is to objectify it, not to grasp it in its own inner reality but to reduce it to the very limited way in which it appears *to us*. For example, the city of Cairo forms an unconscious background for all those who live there. Any statement we might make about this city, or any account we give of it or map we make of it, is according to Heidegger far poorer than the city as it is unconsciously lived. In short, to see something "as" such-and-such is to reduce its manifold reality to a small set of limited properties, which both illuminates and caricatures whatever it is we talk about. In his view, this is what theory does. Theory never encounters things, but only things "as" things. This is the level on which much of continental philosophy is stranded: the difference between a rich, implicit layer of dark pretheoretical experience, and a luminous but impoverished plane of explicit awareness. Managing and commenting on this gap is what hermeneutics aims to do, and it can be said with only a bit of exaggeration that continental philosophy *has become* hermeneutic philosophy. The human being is immersed in a mysterious world of unspoken usages and tries to come to terms with these by interpreting them. In this way, continental philosophy remains human-centered, just as the usual reading of Heidegger wishes it to be.

But here is the problem. It is not only *theory* that objectifies the world, caricatures it, or reduces it to a small number of properties in comparison with its inscrutable implicit depth. Praxis does this every bit as much. Let's say that we all enter the same cramped barroom, stumbling over the cluttered furniture as we go. Let's say that we are all so excited by a discussion we are having that we barely notice the barroom or its furnishings. None of us are objectifying the room theoretically, and so all of us ought to be on an equal footing, and ought to be simply using it in its pretheoretical reality. The problem is that the pretheoretical room is already different for each of us. For one thing, each of us is of different physical constitution, and will have to adjust our posture to the room differently from all of our friends: some of us may find it cramped and cold, while others may sense that it is too hot. Each of us is already in a different mood, so even if we never objectify the room theoretically, each of us is already tacitly objectifying the room as "promising" or "gloomy". The barroom may feel vastly different for customers and employees, for women and men, drinkers and non-drinkers, for those who dominate the conversation and those who are afraid to participate. And this is to say nothing of any dogs, ants, or wasps that may pass through the room. It is the same room for all of us, and yet each of us already comes into relation with in a totally different way, long before any theoretical objectification takes place.

But let's not lose the thread. My point is that the difference between theory and praxis, or between conspicuous object and background horizon, can never be radical enough to do justice to the reality of *things*. If theory cuts practical action down to size, exaggerating and caricaturing it, practical action already does the same. Here too, the barroom has a far deeper reality than can possibly be exhausted by any human, dog, or ant. Even unconscious praxis sometimes overstates the case, misses the point, or fails to grasp what it is dealing with. It is not only theory that sees the thing from outside, reducing it to a set of external qualities. Every one of our actions do this: no two-year-old and no beetle will ever experience a library the same way I do, but neither will I be able to appreciate a rattle fully or explore the spaces under a sidewalk.

Furthermore it is not only humans, dogs, and insects who objectify reality with their actions. The same is even true of inanimate things. When two rocks slam together in distant space, we can assume that they are not "aware" of each other. And yet it is quite clear that they objectify each other anyway: the two asteroids do not fully come into contact with all of the properties of the other. If one asteroid is green and the other red, this will probably be irrelevant to the collision. And yet it is far from irrelevant to the light waves bombarding the rocks, since some wavelengths of light are reflected by one and not the other. Even in a relation between two lumps of sheer matter, objectification will occur.

Every object populating the world encounters millions of other objects at any given moment, each responding to it in its own way, none of them ever fully sounding its depths. The same tree is multiplied into countless perspectives by all the various people who look at it from different angles and in different moods, by the insects that swarm to chew on it, by the drops of water sucked into its trunk. The tree itself is not reducible to any of these perspectives. And neither is it reducible to the *sum total* of them. There are features of the Mediterranean Sea that no currently existing fish is equipped to measure, though a new species could always evolve: perhaps there are strange magnetic forces that exist only in the Mediterranean and nowhere else in the world, and maybe this lost fact was crucial only to a dinosaur species now extinct. To describe the reality of a thing, irreducible to any of its relations or qualities, I can think of no better term than the traditional word *substance*.There is no need to jump to hasty conclusions about what this substance might be. The point is that Heidegger's tool-analysis does not show us that praxis comes before theory. More puzzlingly, it shows that reality comes before quality. The key opposition is not between implicit and explicit, but between substance and relation. With this step, we are faced with the reality of objects that also exist independently of any giant network that tries to objectify them. And in this way, the cardinal tenets of continental philosophy are abandoned. It may be good to review the three principal results of all this:

1. Whereas Heideggerians hold that the usefulness of objects for humans precedes their independent reality, it is clearly the reverse. The point of the tool-analysis is that reality always runs deeper than any objectification. This is the entire point of the theme of being itself, and of the being of specific entities. Along with the fact that a thing is not reducible to its presence-at-hand for a human observer, it is also not reducible to how it presents itself to practical activity. The substance of a thing, whatever it is, must precede its functional form, since the thing is never exhausted by all that does, and since it can support several usages at the same time.[58] Those Heideggerians who scoff at "naive realism" are guilty of something even worse: "naive *relationalism*".

2. Continental philosophers invariably prefer total systems of meaning from which individual objects or words are seen to be nothing more than abstractions. It is necessary to reject this aspect of continental philosophy for a similar reason to the one just stated. To treat an object primarily as part of a network is to assume it can be reduced to that set of qualities and relations that it manifests in this *particular* network. But I have already argued that any object far exceeds the interactions it has with other things in any given moment. Objects, not networks, ought to be the primary topic of continental philosophy: whatever objects might turn out to be, which remains a mystery for now.

3. Finally, the difference between unconscious use and conscious awareness is insufficiently fundamental. Instead of a single privileged gap between human and world, around which philosophy would have to be locked in permanent orbit, there are actually trillions of gaps: or rather, an infinite number. When a dust-mote slams into a marble column, the relationship between these two objects is every bit as puzzling as that between a scholar and a papyrus text. Continental philosophy still suffers from a transcendental hangover, and this leads it to disdain physical causality as philosophically uninteresting. This

attitude is unjustified. All relations are equally puzzling, not just those that involve humans. An increasing number of continental philosophers have proposed (accurately enough) that the name of the movement be changed to "hermeneutic philosophy", in honor of the widely shared commitment to the model of an interpreting human embedded in a dark and rich background. But this only reveals the lingering human-centered bias of the continental school. What is needed is not more hermeneutic philosophy, but more object-oriented philosophy. It remains unclear just what objects are, but it is already clear that they far exceed the human-centered and narrowly holistic prison in which most Heideggerians try to confine them.

With these three points, the Heideggerian orthodoxy is turned on its head. The focus on human praxis and networks of significance reverses, by way of the tool-analysis, into a puzzled reflection on the reality of objects in and of themselves: quite apart from any objectification of them by other objects such as humans, butterflies, or minerals. Unless it follows this lead, continental philosophy will remain stuck in a hermeneutic dead end, a place where in my view little more remains to be accomplished in this tradition. What must be studied is the object, which is... I know not what. However, that is not yet the end of the story: a few more interesting things can be said about objects. In order to avoid confusion with other conceptions of what an object is, we might also use the word "tool-being" as a reminder that the present concept emerges from Heidegger's famous tool-analysis. What do we already know about tool-beings, aside from the fact that they are irreducible to any objectification, whether by humans, animals, plants, or stones?

One thing we obviously know is that tool-beings are loaded with unexpressed qualities. If an object is always a vast surplus beyond its relations of the moment, it has to be asked how those as-yet unexpressed qualities are stored up for the future. There are numerous controversies that might arise here, but I will confine myself to a negative remark: the concept of "potential" should be avoided wherever possible. To say that an acorn is a potential oak tree is clearly true, but the real question is this: what *actual* aspect of the acorn allows it to be potentially an oak tree? To talk about an object in terms of potential is really to view it from the outside, in terms of some future relations it might have, and this enables one to dodge the question of what the actuality of unexpressed qualities might be, here and now. One could argue that unexpressed qualities are only potential, that they have no actuality here and now at all, but I tried to argue against this with my reading of the tool-analysis. I am convinced that objects far exceed their interactions with other objects, and the question is both *what* this excess is, and *where* it is. In any case, these questions are far from new, since they in large part dominated the philosophy of the Renaissance. Well before Leibniz wrote of the still unexpressed qualities enfolded inside of monads, Nicholas of Cusa and Giordano Bruno had done the same, and with perhaps even greater eloquence.

A second point I would like to make about substance is that there seem to be problems with the classical view, for which we can use Aristotle and Leibniz as examples. Briefly put: for these classical philosophers, substance is always substance and relation is always relation. Any particular thing in the world can either be a substance, or an aggregate stemming from relations, but never both in different contexts. I think this is wrong. You may recall that both Aristotle and Leibniz, unlike John Locke, find it impossible to give the name of substance to artificial things such as machines. This, of course, is because they take "nature" as their standard. Since a computer had to be pieced together out of parts, Aristotle would say that it is an arbitrary fabrication rather than a natural unit, and therefore cannot be any sort of substratum for further qualities. In the case of Leibniz it is even easier to understand his fear of granting the name of substance to strange unions of bizarre things, since for Leibniz a substance must always be immortal, a problem that does not haunt Locke. For Leibniz an army cannot be a substance, and neither can a circle of men holding hands, or a pair of diamonds, or the Dutch East India Company. For Aristotle and Leibniz, the roster of substances is somehow fixed; no human will be able to make one. But there is no need to define substance in terms either of nature or immortality. If we define it along the lines of the tool-analysis, a substance is simply that unknown reality of a thing that resists being exhausted by any perceptions of it or relations with it. In this way, we get a much more interesting picture: the world is laced with countless objects which are both substances and relations at the same time.

In one sense the McDonald's Corporation is a vast network of employees, infrastructure, sacks of food ingredients, and circulating cash, none of them reducible to the use that McDonald's makes of them. In another sense this company is a unified actor that has its own reality irreducible to any customer's experience of it or any media complaints about it. We can move in either direction and show that no point in the chain is either solely substance or solely relation: there is a sense in which fried potatoes are integers, discrete chunks of easily manipulated food-units. But there is another sense in which they are vast networks of swirling chemicals. No one point in the chain is uniquely substance, and no one point is uniquely equipped to explain the others. If there really is a tiniest particle, its structure will be of no more use in explaining the total reality of a potato or a corporate entity then they would be in explaining it in reverse. Just as no point in the chain is substance, no point can be called "matter": carbon may be matter compared to the form of a potato, but it is form compared to the matter known as quarks. Every level of reality seems to be two-faced: each is both a real thing and a fabrication that brings other things into relation; each is both a form that unifies its constituents and a matter from which other substances may be built. A corollary of this is that there is no such thing as a mere accident or mere relation. Any relation forms a kind of new reality which could represent a kind of inscrutable substance viewed in different ways by numerous other realities. There is no such thing as relation: the world is utterly jam-packed with substances, some of them very strange, some of them extremely short-lived. This standpoint differs from Aristotle and Leibniz in not allowing an honor roll of types of objects that count as substances (horses, trees) while disdaining others (circuses, electric cable, professional sports teams). It differs from natural science in insisting on the metaphysical status of form rather than the supposed explanatory power of physical matter. Another way of saying this is that the difference between primary and secondary qualities strikes me as false. Are the physical properties of bulk and texture any more real than sensations of sweet and sour? I don't see it.

A third aspect of the problem is one that I find a bit unnerving, but still compelling. I have suggested that one substance never exhausts another, never fully comes in contact with another. But the full truth is even more disturbing than this: no substance ever comes in contact with another at all. When two rocks slam into one another, what two things are actually encountering one another? I have already said that the rocks encounter caricatures of one another, nothing more, since the unfathomable rock-reality is never fully tapped by any sort of relation. But this causes problems, because it means that by definition no two substances can ever interact. There must be some third term that allows them to communicate. Historically this doctrine is known as occasional cause (rarely taken seriously, though it was crucially important for both Islamic philosophy and seventeenth century European thought). It seems to me that if what I said about substances is correct, then there is no way to avoid some sort of theory of occasional cause. However, occasionalism is strongly associated with the specific theory that God is what allows all substances to interact. This theory is unlikely to satisfy even religiously minded philosophers in our time, so let's drop the term "occasional cause" and speak instead of "vicarious cause". In some strange way, substances must be able to affect each other vicariously rather than directly. Do they do this by means of yet another substance, or is there some other force in the cosmos that is still missing from the model I have described? I still do not know the answer to this.

There is one last paradox that ought to be mentioned here. A substance or tool-being is supposed to be that which exists independently of all relations: Cairo or Beirut as irreducible to any views of them; the sun as irreducible to its beneficial effects on any particular square inch of the solar system, and even as irreducible to the sum total of these. One very obvious question arises if we consider highly strange and arbitrary possible substances, such as the one that links France, the planet Mars, a few syringes, and all the atoms of lead in Brazil. There seems to be nothing to stop me from calling this monstrous child "Substance X" and claiming that it really exists. If someone objects that Substance X is unreal simply because it never has any effects on the outer world, I would be unable to use this criterion even if I wished to do so, since I have already said that external efficacy is precisely not the nature of substance, which is supposed to rest in itself, independently of all relations. So I am also not sure how we build metaphysical firewalls to prevent the creation of absurd substances, without contradicting ourselves by using an external criterion of reality.

Let's leave it at that for today. My first purpose was to show that even though Heidegger is usually seen as the very pillar of the anti-metaphysical attitude among continentals, his tool-analysis opens the door to a bizarre new metaphysical realism. My second purpose was to sketch a few unusual and perplexing features of this realism, which although far removed from the intellectual culture of continental philosophy, might conceivably lead to a revival of metaphysics within that culture: someday, not too far away.

8. Physical Nature and the Paradox of Qualities (2006)

This lecture was given on 21 April, 2006 in Reykjavik, Iceland at the annual meeting of the Nordic Society for Phenomenology. Interesting things were afoot. My reading material on this trip was Quentin Meillassoux's now famous book Après la finitude, *which had only recently been published. Ray Brassier, who had invited me to speak at Middlesex University in London the previous year, had recently returned from a visit to Paris, seen the book on sale there, and suggested it was something I might enjoy. From 15-17 April, while in Akureyri on the northern coast of Iceland, I exchanged numerous e-mails with Brassier about my positive impression of Meillassoux's book, and it was during these discussions that he suggested a group event featuring the three of us and Iain Hamilton Grant. I immediately sent messages of inquiry to both Grant and Meillassoux, and thus was born "the movement", which only received the name of Speculative Realism the following year. The Iceland lecture itself is interesting for several reasons, but primarily for its link between physical causation and the inner drama of Husserl's intentional objects. The distinction it draws between real and intentional objects was received with friendly bewilderment by the largely Husserlian audience that day.*

Most schools of present-day philosophy are united in celebrating the death of metaphysics. Phenomenology is no exception. But in the brief paper that follows, I will try to show that Husserl's model of intentional objects is deeply enmeshed in metaphysical themes that cannot be escaped. More than this, it is Husserl who accidentally grants us the resources to revive philosophic concern with physical nature: or more generally, with the metaphysics of objects, whether human, animal, angelic, vegetable, plastic, or stone. Furthermore, despite his relative lack of interest in the history of metaphysics and his wish to wipe the slate clean and begin with a newly scientific philosophy, Husserl's intentional objects brush up against classical themes treated by the occasionalist metaphysics dominant at various times among the Arabs and the French. I will begin with Heidegger, pass to Husserl, turn toward some brief remarks on occasionalism in general, and close with a meditation on the inner volcanic structure of objects. The result will be as follows: physical nature must be approached by considering the paradoxical structure of qualities.

1. Real Objects

According to the conventional view, Husserl walled off a space for phenomenology by asking us to ignore the natural reality of objects, focusing instead on how they are given to consciousness. In this way he allowed philosophy to take a distance from the naiveté of science and metaphysics, and built the arena in which rigorous philosophy becomes possible. Heidegger's tool-analysis then showed the limitations of this approach, by showing that objects are used before they are seen. In this way, it is said, Heidegger pointed to a shadowy equipmental background withdrawn from the sphere of lucid awareness. I will in fact endorse this conventional view. But I will also urge that it be radicalized in three different ways. In so doing, we will ironically be led back toward Husserl, who in some ways can teach us more than Heidegger about the relations between one object and another.

First, we need to abandon the persistent yet shallow idea that Heidegger's tool-analysis subordinates theory to praxis. It is true enough that staring at a hammer or making theories about it fails to capture the genuine reality of this hammer as we go about using it. Yes, the hammer is assigned to numerous systems of purposes and finalities, and when we gaze at the hammer theoretically we reduce it to a caricature, ripping it from the world in which it is deeply involved. But this is only half the story. For human praxis turns the tool into a caricature no less than theory does. My grabbing and manipulating of a screwdriver or power drill also fail to grasp the total reality of these objects. My handling of these items can be surprised by their inner reality or be resisted by it just as much as my explicit awareness can. All human relations to objects strip them of their inner depth, revealing only some of their qualities to view. This has only rarely been seen by Heidegger commentators, but was already recognized by Bergson and others, who recognized quite early that to use a thing is no more intimate a relation with its depths than to see it. Both approaches to the thing reduce it to a series of superficial profiles far removed from the object in its withering interior activity, which can never be fully exhausted by any human means. That is the first way in which Heidegger's tool-analysis must be radicalized.

The second step will seem strange, though it is also inevitable. Namely, it is not just human relations to objects that cut them down to size by reducing them to outer contours and profiles of their inner reality. Instead, relationality in general does this. It is not some special feature of the human psyche or human deeds that turns a thing into a caricature. This reduction belongs to any relation between any two objects in the universe, no matter what they may be. My perception of fire and cotton fails to use up the total realities of these beings, since they are describable at infinite length in a way that I can never approach. We have seen that the same is true of my use of these objects for practical tasks. But more generally, the fire and cotton also fail to make full contact with *each other* when they touch, despite their uniting in a bond of destruction that takes no heed of the colors and scents that humans or animals may detect emanating from both of them. In other words, objects withdraw from each other and not just from humans. In this respect, human beings are just one more type of object among trillions of others in the cosmos. As I have argued elsewhere and at length, Heidegger's famous distinction between ready-to-hand and present-at-hand is not about a difference between practical handy tools and sparkling lucid perceptions, but entails a more general difference between objects and relations. Presence *means* relationality, nothing more. To consider an object in its being means to consider it in its withdrawal from all forms of presence, whether as something seen, used, or just spatially present among other entities. All objects withdraw from each other, not just from humans. This is the second radicalization of Heidegger's tool-analysis. But we now seem to be as distant as possible from phenomenology, since we have descended into the leper colonies of nature and metaphysics that Husserl had urged us to avoid.

And yet, a third radicalization pushes us away from Heidegger and back toward Husserl. For if cotton and fire withdraw from each other no less than from humans, it needs to be asked how they can interact at all. The duel of inanimate entities seems to involve a sort of occasional cause, given the mutual withdrawal of objects that are now turned into concealed dark crystals of reality. What, then, is the real cause that unites them? We cannot say God, as in early Islamic theology and seventeenth century Europe, since this explains nothing as long as the divine mechanisms are left in darkness. But neither can it be the human mind arbitrarily bundling together discrete qualities into a fictional underlying substance, as is the case for many of the empiricists, since this unjustifiably reduces objects to the way we experience them. And we will soon see that despite his bracketing of the natural world, Husserl does not reduce objects to our experience of objects. Nonetheless, the bracketing does have an effect. I am not among those who contend that Husserl already anticipated the tool-analysis in his own works. For given that intentional objects have a merely ideal existence having no traffic with a real universe of unleashed causal powers, he deserves to be called an idealist, and this title ought to be fairly uncontroversial. By contrast, Heidegger tacitly lays claim to a real cosmos filled with objects in the form of surprising real forces irreducible to any relationality at all. The problem is that Heidegger only allows objects to withdraw from human Dasein, never from each other as well. For this reason, he never reaps the dividends of the weird realism he inaugurates.

2. Intentional Objects

The great breakthrough of phenomenology would have been impossible without suspending natural objects from consideration. It was important to move from a hazy notion of solid billiard balls unleashing forces against each other to a more rigorous foundation in how things actually present themselves to us. The cost of this step was high, since nature and metaphysics were summarily booted from a human-centered realm of conscious acts. This exaggerated view of real objects as something inherently unphilosophical is what opened the door to Heidegger's shadowy, withdrawn tool-beings.

Yet it was never the case that Husserl simply opposed human experience to an unknowable landscape of natural physical solids. For in an obvious sense, Husserl is no empiricist at all. In *Logical Investigations* II we find his marvelous assault on the perceptual theories of Locke, Berkeley, and Hume. The guiding insight of his attack is the same in all of these cases: humans do not intend "experienced contents", as if everything we dealt with lay patent before our eyes. The alternative endorsed by Husserl is that we intend *objects*. These are not the natural objects of the sciences, reducible to physical matter or fields of force; neither are they the unnatural tool-objects of Heidegger, withdrawing into silent subterranean execution. Instead they are the famous "intentional objects", which have no more place in Heidegger than in British Empiricism. For Heidegger, if there are objects they can only lie in a shadowy depth, not in the midst of perception itself.

Intentional objects are not to be identified with real ones in the least, and for several reasons. For one thing, they are merely ideal and may not exist at all. The real object "fire" scalds, burns, boils, melts, and cracks other real objects, while the intentional object "fire" has a very different function: it merely unifies a shifting set of profiles and surfaces whose various flickerings never affect its underlying ideal unity. Real objects withdraw. But intentional objects do not withdraw, even though they never become entirely visible or utterly fulfilled in perception. The contrast is important. Whereas the real tree forever recedes into its underground reality, untouchable by anything else in the cosmos, the intentional tree is always fully there before us. Although it may taunt us with the endless supply of angles and distances from which it can be viewed, and is never seen in all its profiles simultaneously, there is another sense in which the intentional tree is always completely fulfilled from the start. After all: there it is, the tree, and we are now all thinking about it. What remains unfulfilled is merely its sensuous content, while the tree-object as such is already fully manifest. If we call the real object *withdrawn*, so that too little of its being is present, we might call the intentional object *encrusted*, in the sense that too much of its being is present. For the intentional object is always covered with inessential surface effects that must be scraped away through eidetic variation, so as to move closer toward the more austere essence lying beneath.

Finally, there is the most important difference of all between real and intentional objects. Real objects are sliced apart into private, mutually exclusive vacuums, with none of them ever touching their neighbors. By contrast, there is a sense in which intentional objects pass gradually into one another. Like textile pigments, intentional objects *bleed* into one another. Or alternatively, like open bottles of wine or linen shirts, they *breathe* into their environment. Although it is true that I am able to distinguish tree, rock, and soil entirely from one another in a single perception, it is nonetheless true that each of these intentional objects is so encrusted with inessential sensuous features that a great deal of labor is required for the phenomenologist to approach their essences.

To repeat, although Husserl seems to begin his philosophy by putting objects out of the picture, he restores them to the throne in the form of intentional objects. It should be noted that this step not only amounts to an attack on the British Empiricists, for whom he never had much sympathy anyway. More than this, it also marks a daring reform of the concepts of his teacher Brentano. In *Logical Investigations* V he modifies Brentano's thesis that all intentionality is based in presentations to say that all are based in "object-giving acts" that are always beyond mere presentation. In another interesting twist, Husserl uses the phrase "nominal acts" as a synonym for object-giving acts. Just as a proper name (for Saul Kripke) continues to point rigidly to a single unitary thing despite all variations in that thing's known attributes, an intentional object rests like the Sphinx amidst the sandstorms of various qualities that rage around its slumbering form.

But here we reach the central problem of this paper: the *paradoxical* structure of qualities. For it is not just that we have intentional objects on one side and sensuous qualities on the other, in a kind of permanent dualism (at least not in the *Logical Investigations*). That would come too close to the neo-Kantian distinction between sensibility and understanding that Husserl openly rejects. Instead, every supposed speck of sensuous or carnal data is already shaped into objective form. There is no red that is not the red of an apple, cherry, wine, or exploding giant star. Any time we try to step back to a point where we might observe purely given colors and shapes, à la the empiricists, we find that Husserl leaves us no room to do so. Everything already points toward intentional objects. There is no pre-given blur of sense data that then gets molded into tangible units. Everything appears in intentional acts, and intentionality is always and only object-giving. Yet intentional objects never appear except by way of some contour or face. What then are these contours and faces? What do the senses actually encounter, given that we do not merely stretch out toward elusive intentional objects, but actually stand somewhere in particular, amidst some buzz or drone in the air, some kaleidoscopic whirl of visual effects? This is the paradox of perceptual qualities. At the close of this paper I will suggest that the same paradox lies at the heart of causation as well.

3. Occasional Cause

Despite the different sorts of warnings against metaphysics made by Husserl and Heidegger, we already stand in the midst of it. Heidegger's real objects lead us into metaphysics due to their impossible isolation from each other. If hammers, rocks, and flames withdraw from all other entities, then it needs to be explained why anything happens in the world at all. In this sense, Heidegger faces the same problem as the various Arab and French occasionalists. Occasionalism, well-known as the theory that God intervenes directly at all moments in every grain of dust in the cosmos, even recreating the universe afresh in every instant of time, is generally viewed as a minor historical curio to be pored over by monks and archivists. But in fact, occasionalism is a far broader problem than is usually believed. The key to occasionalism is not the rather dated and arbitrary theology that would have God meddle in everything that occurs. Instead, the key is that things in the world exist only side-by-side, not bleeding into one another. And this "side-by-side" is what links the empiricists (even when they are atheists) to full-blown occasionalist theology. As Steven Nadler rightly observes,[59] there is a striking similarity in the arguments of such vastly different figures as the Islamic firebrand al-Ash'ari, the punished anti-

Aristotelian Nicolas d'Autrecourt, the devout Catholic Malebranche, and the impious David Hume. In all of these philosophies, one object or one quality is unable to link directly to another. Unfortunately, all of them make a single hypocritical exception. For the theologians it is of course God who is able to break the side-by-side principle and let His power link the things. For the empiricists it is the human soul which exerts the hypocritical power by bundling separate qualities into a supposed underlying substratum that probably isn't even there. But hypocrisy is no solution. Instead, we should bite the bullet in each individual case and not look to some magical super-entity to link withdrawn objects together, whether it be almighty God or the almighty human mind. Each individual object must be equipped to touch and jostle others *despite* withdrawing from those others.

Then occasionalism is a philosophy of externality, with things existing side-by-side without bleeding or breathing into one another. This may take the form of impotent fire and cotton never acting without God's intervention, or perhaps it will be expressed instead in the empiricist maxim "relations are external to their terms". But whereas real objects trap us in an occasionalist deadlock in their cryptic mutual withdrawal, intentional objects already bleed and breathe, one phasing into another without difficulty. Furthermore, the intentional object somehow already achieves the godlike effect of blending countless profiles, halos, masks, and veils into a single intentional object, packing numerous qualities into a single essence even as they somehow remain separate qualities. For this reason perhaps the problem of occasional causation can be solved by looking to the field of perception, and then in some way moving back to the zone of real objects. I will now make a brief attempt to do so. The problem is important not only for clarifying Heidegger or Husserl (in however unorthodox a fashion) but also for elucidating numerous central problems of classical metaphysics. For occasional cause, which we can rename *vicarious cause* so as to avoid needless theological overtones, is nothing less than the problem of how things can be both separate and linked. And this problem lies at the root of famous classical oppositions such as the one and the many, identity and difference, and the opposition between substance on the one hand and aggregates, accidents, relations, and qualities on the other.

4. The Volcanic Core of Objects

My thesis, which will sound strange at first, is that everything in the world happens only on the *interior* of objects. Since objects cannot touch one another directly they must be able to interact only within some sort of vicarious medium that contains each of them. The inside of an object can be viewed as a volcano, kaleidoscope, witch's cauldron, steel mill, or alchemist's flask in which one thing is somehow converted into another. It is not difficult to show why this must be the case. Let's start with the ambiguity lying in intentional acts. Husserl openly admits that our intention of an object is in a certain sense *one*, but in another sense *two*. It is not just as if two entities were sitting side-by-side; rather, the intentional act forms a union from the start. On the other hand, since the tree or flower and I do not fuse together into some colossal glacier without parts, we must also admit that each of the components of the act still somehow remains separate from the other.

Now, there is no choice but to call this unified act an object in its own right. Not because it is made of atoms or stone or metallic ore; not because it lasts for millions of years; not because it can be picked up and thrown like a ball or a firecracker. No, the intentional object is an object for the same reason as any other object: namely, it is a reality whose full depths can never be exhaustively probed. My intention of a chimney, pirate ship, or avalanche provides endless fuel for *ad nauseam* description by phenomenologists or by Marcel Proust. But since we have spoken of two kinds of objects, it is important to clarify what kind of object the intentional act is. And here, note that the unified intentional act can only be a *real* object, not just an intentional one. My relation to the tree is not something just viewed by others, nor even something just viewed by myself. Instead, I am *actively deployed* in contending with this tree or this mountain right now, even if they turn out to be illusory. The result of this is strange. The intentional object and I both somehow reside in the inner molten core of a *real* object, the total intentional act. This gives new meaning to the old phrase "intentional *in*existence." It is not just that phenomena exist as the contents of a mental sphere. Rather, mental life and its acts are both contained within a larger object in some still undetermined way.

But this is not just a story of human perception. In other words, it is not just the poignantly unique features of human being that place intentionality on the interior of an object. We cannot know exactly what an inanimate object experiences. We cannot be sure whether Leibniz was right to compare the perceptions of a rock to those of a very dizzy human, or whether we should speak of "experience" at all in the inanimate realm. At the moment, it is hard even to imagine a theory able to clarify more precisely the differences between humans, dolphins, pineapples, chairs, and atoms.

However, I would propose that if we look closely at intentionality, the key to it lies not in some special human *cogito* marked by lucid representational awareness. Instead, what is most striking about intentionality is the object-giving encounter. In other words, human alertness stands amidst a swarm of concrete sensual realities. But contra British Empicirism, it encounters objects rather than raw qualities, since qualities never make any sense except as a radiation or odor emanating from intentional objects. This must also hold true for the inanimate realm. For just as raw qualities cannot exist in the human sphere, the world of possibly soulless matter also cannot unfold amidst dots of barely determinate color or heat. One object always encounters another object, albeit never in fully exhaustive form.

To summarize, *every* relation must form an object: one in which its components are somehow pressed against each other, encountering one another in more or less turbulent fashion, even while something links them more stably from above. Whether the converse is also true (namely, whether every object is also composed of relations) is an interesting question indeed, since it involves the problem of whether there can be an infinite regress of objects wrapped in objects sealed in objects frozen in objects, or whether we reach some ultimate atomic point of reality. This problem will have to be dealt with elsewhere.

It should be admitted that there is an asymmetry in the intentional relationship between me and the objects that I witness. But the asymmetry in question is not that of "lucid conscious agent versus stupid block of inanimate matter." Instead, the asymmetry is simply that in this case I am the one doing the intending, and the object may not be encountering me at all: not out of inanimate stupidity, but simply because I may have no effect on it. The point can be seen more clearly if we imagine two people staring at each other. Clearly we have two intentional acts here, not one. If intentionality unfolds on the inside of some object, as claimed earlier, then we will have to speak of two separate objects. But when we intend, note that we cannot be described as the "active" ones, even if it is we who must engage in a frenzy of perceptual arrangements. On the contrary it is I who am the passive one, since it is I who have been drawn into a new space by the object I encounter.

We have now arrived at the molten inner core of objects as the place where reality unfolds. It is the one site where relations and events might occur, and the only point of reality that is filled with the sparkle of concrete perception rather than withdrawing into cryptic, inscrutable distance. Put differently, Heidegger's *real* objects, the tool-beings that surpass any relation that one might have to them, seem unable to relate to each other at all. Each is trapped in its own private vacuum of reality. And this pushes Heidegger in the direction of occasionalism, since he is left with no way to explain how one thing affects another. By contrast, Husserl's intentional objects, for which there is surprisingly no equivalent in Heidegger's mature phase, do *nothing but* melt and bleed together in consciousness. For the intentional object is all too easily encrusted with sunlight, shadow, and other accidental surface-effects that proclaim its essence without forming part of it. Hence it seems that the field of intentionality is the furnace in which the labors of the world are accomplished. In other words, the solution to the problem of how objects relate is found on the core of objects themselves. The problem that remains to be solved is how one object ever breaks into the core of another. If this did not happen we would be left with nothing but countless private universes, none communicating with any other.

Before moving on, it might be asked what is accomplished by turning toward the interior of objects as the site of reality. The most important result is to have eliminated the idea of a special human transcendence, rising above the world into some windy and starry space from which the things can be seen "as" what they are. Humans do not rise above the world but only burrow ever more deeply into it, digging down toward the heart of things by *fusing* with them. We always stand somewhere.

But even a heremeneutical approach to phenomenology would already claim to know this, conceding that "of course" humans only perceive from amidst certain presuppositions or from a distinct corporeal or historical stance. But this is not enough. For even if we replace the lucid, transcendent cogito with a murkier, more cryptic human thrown into its historico-linguistic surroundings, there is still a fixation on a single unique rift or correspondence between human and world. The human/world relation is treated as extra special, different in kind from the relation of cotton and fire. This is the heritage that must be abandoned. Instead, we should be willing to say that any relation between any two things at all is on the same footing. There are levels of the world, and the human being can only move up or down between them, exploring all the contours of the world that exist with or without our awareness, and not claim to be the unique fissure across which reality unfolds. Consciousness is no longer special, but just a special case of the relation between part and whole.

But now we approach the conclusion, and it is difficult and provisional. The initial problem is this: intentionality ought to encounter nothing but objects, since the whole point of *Logical Investigations* II was that the empiricists were wrong to claim there is any surface "given" of experience. Objects are never fully given. But how can they even be *partially* given, since any of the surface qualities by which a thing is manifest should also be an intentional object in its own right? Whenever we try to retreat from the not-fully-presented chair or aluminum can to the sensual data in which it becomes accessible, we find that there is no data. To speak of some raw, dough-like matter that would then be shaped into objects by categorial intuition is to retreat into a distinction between sensibility and understanding that Husserl's *Second Investigation* aimed to destroy. In short, the problem is how we can experience anything at all. Why do we not hover silently in a black void, cut off from everything and perceiving nothing?

The answer of course is that intentional objects do not withdraw, but are simply *encrusted* with things that do not belong to their essence. The lingering notion that an intentional tree could in any way be hidden is probably linked to an overly *visual* reading of intentionality: "I only see one side of the tree right now, but there are other sides now invisible to me," as if some massive armada of cubist perspectives could add up to the essence of a thing. In fact, the essence of the thing ought to be discernible without any of these perspectives at all, since they are mere encrustations that have more to do with the light and breeze surrounding the tree than with the intentional tree itself. Intentional objects are never hidden, but simply illuminated with too many lights, salted with too many spices, clothed in too many costumes. They must be stripped progressively bare if we are to know what really belongs to them.

In the intentional field, objects bleed together in ways that muddy the essences of each. Two trees blend together into one at a distance, or transient moonlight gives us false expectations about the color of a distant thing. The goal of eidetic variation (as of most human intelligence) is simply to separate the wheat from the chaff, the essential from the accidental, thereby reversing the mixture or bleeding with which the senses begin. As Merleau-Ponty shows, and already William James, the very movement of our bodies, with its minute adjustments of posture and tiltings of the head and slight squinting or opening of the mouth to hear, is an instrument for approaching the object in just the right way to capture it in its most flattering or revealing light. As James notes, there is a proper distance from which every object ought to be seen: a book would be ridiculous if pressed directly against our faces, or if attempts were made to read it at one hundred meters. The same holds true for all objects at a various range of possible distances. Moreover, Aristotle already observed that *memory* makes this same split for us: we remember the river as an object, not the river with all its shimmering surface distortions, which memory subtracts from the phenomenon as initially presented. In any case, perception and theory try to filter out the accidents of the thing and present it in its essential nature. In this way, perception, theory, and memory all reverse the work of the senses.

But there is a problem. For even if we call certain qualities of an object "essential", they are not yet the thing itself. For each of the thing's qualities are separate from each other, and we do not arrive at the thing by piecing them all together. The thing, beyond all its *essential* qualities, is more like a brooding power or style that lurks beneath the qualities and animates them. It is interesting to recall that Husserl described intentional acts as nominal acts. For this is what proper names do, as seen most recently in Kripke's school, but as already described by Husserl and even Aristotle. To call out a name ("Paul!"; "Yara!") is not to call out to essential qualities lying beneath all the accidental ones. To say "tree" or "moon" is not to point to any perceptual qualities in particular, since any of these may be falsifiable. When Rimabud writes: "in the forest there is a clay pit with a nest of white animals", the force of this line does not come from its accurate description of the scene's essential qualities. His poem would not be ruined if the poet were initially mistaken and the true state of affairs were one of beige animals living in mud. In short, with names we go not just beyond *accidents*, but even beyond *essential* qualities, calling out to some ghostly style that inhabits the world in a never quite definable way. And with this step we seem to move beyond the sphere of intentional objects and toward real ones. Instead of merely reversing the work of the senses, we now seem to be reversing the work of causation itself, since we are pointing to a lonely object in the distance and no longer in its relation to us.

For this sort of pointing, let's use the general term "allure", for a thing becomes alluring when it seems to be a ghostly power exceeding any of its lists of properties, one that animates those properties from within by means of some ill-defined demonic energy. Allure splits an object from its qualities. This happens not just in the act of naming, but in countless different cases, all of them carrying a strong emotional charge. We see it in metaphor, in which "man is a wolf" (Max Black's well-known example) seems to split the human from his qualities and replace them with wolf-qualities. We see it in humor, where the comic dupe seems to have no free and easy connection with his face or legs any longer, looking stupid with a giant red nose or while slipping on the ice. We see it in beauty, where the beautiful thing sparkles and recedes, hard to define by any list of specific beautiful qualities. We see it in courage, where people stay true to themselves despite the possibly disastrous impending consequences, and in fierce loyalty, where the commitment to a person or cause remains in place even when all their appealing qualities seem to have vanished. We see it also in embarrassment, where the person no longer seems flawlessly in control of his actions, but awkwardly overexerts himself in trying to row a boat or play a round of golf. Perhaps even more interestingly, we also see it in one type of theory: the kind that Thomas Kuhn called *paradigm-shifting* theory. The reign of a paradigm is not socially constructed mob rule, but simply the underlying commitment to a specific model of objects that endures in the face of its remaining paradoxes and even its experimental falsifications. This distinguishes it from the sort of theory that simply mops up erroneous views of what is essential and accidental in the world. To shift a paradigm is to create or discover a new object, one that might be identified by certain typical qualities but is certainly never identical with them.

But notice that allure does not just *reverse* the work of causation, by separating a thing from its surroundings. Allure is also a new act of causation, since it brings me into relation with the new object: whether it be Rimbaud's clay-pit metaphor, Deleuze's concept of the virtual, a new style of artwork, or a fascinating new friend. But allure is not just a *kind* of causation: it *is* causation. Not only is it the sole event that brings two objects together, but both causation and allure (unlike normal theory and perception) have a *binary* structure. Different people may disagree over whether the same joke is funny, and some may find it funnier than others do, but ultimately it is either funny or it is not for me, here and now. Just so, either the fire causes the cotton to burst into flame or it does not. A metaphor either seizes me or it flops completely. Either I am loyal, courageous, or embarrassed at any given moment, or I am not.

In this way, we find a structure at the heart of intentional life that also pertains even to sheer physical causation. Somehow a real object is converted into a merely intentional one, buffered and causally neutralized by being encrusted with various accidents, and ultimately encrusted even with its supposed essential qualities. But sometimes, for reasons that cannot be further explored here, the debris is cleared away and the object is encountered as flickering at a distance, in all its naked allure. In this respect metaphysics may be a branch of aesthetics, and causation merely a form of beauty. In any case, the border is now blurring between ideal or intentional reality and bracketed physical reality. Phenomenology is blurring into metaphysics.

9. Space, Time, and Essence: An Object-Oriented Approach (2008)

This essay was written in the early months of 2008, and was based on a presentation I had given on 23 November, 2007 at the Technical University of Delft, The Netherlands. At that time I was on sabbatical from my position in Cairo and serving as a visiting professor at the University of Amsterdam. In this essay I was struggling toward my current fourfold model of time, space, essence, and eidos. But my notebooks from the period show that the Delft talk had referred only to a threefold of "time," "space," and "?," with no hint of a fourth term. As concerns the reference to young Beatrice in the essay, she is the daughter of friends living in England, and had shown from a young age an inclination toward philosophical questions about space and time. The essay was originally intended for an anthology of articles on space and time; I withdrew it after balking at the editor's demand that it be footnoted, which struck me as inappropriate in this case.

Space and time are of intimate concern to everyone. The whole of our lives unfolds in space and time, as do the wildest fantasies we conceive. To reflect on their paradoxes may even be the quickest route to a philosophical mood. The following pages suggest a fresh approach to these venerable themes. My strategy is to consider space and time indirectly, by way of an apparently different topic: the structure of objects. If this indirect method succeeds, an object-oriented philosophy will allow us to outflank the stale trench warfare that marks so many of the disputes over space and time.

1. Space and Time

Space extends from the provincial town of my birth toward capital cities, mountain ranges, oceans, and the mines and spice routes of foreign nations. The ocean depths are home to bizarre creatures enduring horrific pressures, and the core of the earth might harbor bacteria even stranger than this. Still further away are the moon, the outer planets, and the icy Oort Cloud with its stagnant mist of dim future comets. Telescopes view even remoter places, and beyond the gaze of these instruments are sites more distant than these, some of them grimmer than the plains of Hell. Space is the home of black holes and quasars, but also of Stonehenge, the Serengeti, Las Vegas, and the bones of the Caesars.

Time includes the present moment, which often enough feels heavy and hopeless. Yet it also includes those uncanny past ages when none of us existed, when ancient grandparents cooked or did battle on the immemorial savannah, barely mating in just the right combinations for each of us to appear. Thousands of generations earlier were ancestors so monstrous that we would kill them on sight rather than honoring them. A similar danger may lie in the future: eons hence, our offspring may have evolved into a species more repulsive than any the universe has seen. Shifting from the scale of biology to that of astronomy, we find even remoter past and future times, in which the very structure of matter may be different from the one we know. Yet even without going to such extremes, the space and time of everyday life contains abundant mysteries, however muffled by common sense they may be. We rarely consider it strange that fires now burn somewhere on earth without harming me, that oceans churn but do not drown me, that I cannot smell the sulfur and tar that bubble at this instant in some industrial cauldron in Romania, and that I am currently safe from all extant tigers and cobras. Yet such facts ought to seem wondrous to a philosopher. Similar hidden enigmas arise in connection with time. How uncanny it is that I, now a scholar in Egypt nearing middle age, clearly remember myself as a young brown-haired child surrounded by pets and relatives now deceased, in an Iowa town I rarely visit, in a house reduced to ashes years ago. How much more disturbing to think that someday, this child-adult body will be placed in a grave or a crypt, consumed in a furnace, or devoured by fish or wild animals as a handful of survivors weep over my fate and sift through the remnants of what I did and did not mean to them. Indeed, the melancholic wonders of space and time might spark an entire philosophy. They are the clearest, most basic prod to philosophical reflection that we have.

Children are already capable of such reflections. In fact, they often face these mysteries more resolutely than adults, who are too distracted by battles for supremacy *within* space and time to reflect on these arenas themselves. This was brought to mind recently by a talented five-year-old girl named Beatrice, the daughter of friends in Bournemouth, England. One of her questions in recent months was this: "what's at the end of space?" As her mother informed her, no one knows the answer to this question or plausibly claims to know, though efforts to find out have not been lacking. Neither philosophy, nor physics, nor astronomy, nor Scripture has finished the debate. And though it is quite easy to remember a time when young Beatrice was not yet born, she already poses questions that touch the limits of human understanding. If her question had been "what's at the end of time?", her mother's answer would have been similar. Children might wonder whether time has a beginning and an end, whether it is reversible, and other such things. And in every case their youthful conclusions bear a striking resemblance to those of our greatest intellectual figures, who have little understanding not only of what happened before time, but even of whether the question itself makes sense.

As Beatrice ages, as her evident vocation for the deepest questions of metaphysics sharpens, she will face numerous perils in her development. With respect to space and time her major enemy will not be dogma, since here the lack of certainty is clear to everyone. The more likely dangers are scepticism, demoralization, and the usual bullying by encyclopedic pedants. With so many great thinkers having weighed in on these themes, and with all their disputes so little resolved, it is possible that Beatrice will become discouraged about shedding new light of her own on space and time. Seeing nothing but years of library work ahead, with no clear outcome likely, she may resign herself to an inability to innovate in such matters. Among the range of classic problems connected with space and time, there are several prominent disputes that she might feel especially powerless to advance:

1. Do space and time arise from relations between things, or are they independent containers for entities? This was the subject of the brilliant dispute between Leibniz and Clarke in 1715-16, which was by extension a conflict between Leibniz and his nemesis Isaac Newton.
2. Are space and time made of quantized chunks, or are they smoothly flowing continua? This question sparked the philosophy of Bergson, from his first book in 1889 through his other great works.
3. Are space and time finite or infinite? This question was dismally termed unanswerable by Kant's First Antinomy.
4. Finally, are space and time separate domains, or do they belong instead to a single space-time, as held by Minkowski and Einstein?

2. The Letter to Beatrice

To speak of Leibniz, Clarke, Newton, Bergson, Kant, Minkowski, and Einstein is to invoke an intimidating roster of names. Who could hope to add anything new to the insights of such figures? At best we might hope to collate the insights of these great thinkers, either choosing one of them as our special hero, or coming to a pragmatic, muddled compromise among the best aspects of each. Yet this would distort the aspirations of Beatrice and her young colleagues, who seek a clear and decisive approach to their questions. Now, the father of Beatrice states with admirable modesty that "she's just an ordinary little girl, I suspect all children have these thoughts but probably adults just don't listen to them." But let's imagine for a moment that Beatrice continues to ask these questions with such tenacity that her parents finally realize that she has a special talent for deep speculation. Let's imagine further that, given my acquaintance with her parents and firm interest in metaphysical issues, the parents were to offer me the post of tutoring young Beatrice in matters of space and time: a job no philosopher could ever refuse. But finally, let's also imagine that soon after accepting the offer, I was diagnosed with a mortal illness leaving me weeks from death in some decayed urban hospital. With young Beatrice still only five years old, there is little chance of progress with lessons; in any case, the girl's health would be ill-served by visits to a dying mentor. Hence, the only way of partially fulfilling my promise would be to leave a written testament encouraging the girl and her friends always to think for themselves, no matter what pressures mount over the years. With this written legacy, I would act as a sort of Dante-in-reverse, leading Beatrice from beyond the grave to the highest realms of speculation. For reasons of health and of pedagogy, this final document would have to cover the problems of space and time as economically as possible, in a few dozen pages or less. But this limitation would also be a lucky advantage, since the whole point of the essay is to free Beatrice and her friends from the mountains of erudition that might only discourage their future conceptual gambles.

Though it may sound strange when addressing mere children, the most helpful metaphor here is of a military sort. Intellectuals have long been accustomed to view military leaders as one-dimensional oppressors and killers. This attitude overlooks the admirable *realism* of the military: forces must be massed in specific places, and strategies adapted to the actual nature of the enemy. Our objective is to throw new light on several classical problems of space and time with the greatest possible economy. But at the outset we face nothing but erudition and uncertainty, in perhaps equal amounts. When excessive commentary obscures a basic human problem that fascinates even children, then we have most likely entered a situation of trench warfare. In those historical moments when firepower outstrips mobility, opposing armies find it safer to stay motionless, dug into the earth in a stable, shielded position. The same holds for intellectual firepower and mobility as well. Whenever conceptual innovation comes to a close, the life of the mind is reduced to exchanges of gunfire and cannisters of gas. Millions of lives are expended with no one gaining an inch; boasts are made over body counts, while the frontier itself remains motionless. If Immanuel Kant deserves credit for anything, it is for recognizing the trench-warfare conditions of the metaphysics of his time, with its increasingly pointless proofs and counterproofs. Kant's unfortunate solution was to adopt an agnostic attitude toward the nature of things-in-themselves: the rough equivalent of escaping trench warfare by wearing earplugs. But at least Kant saw the intellectual horror of endless dispute between opposed positions. Trench warfare is just as wasteful a fate for the intellectual as for the soldier.

The lesson for us is clear: we cannot tackle space and time frontally. Much like Ulysses S. Grant in the 1860s, we are butchers when making direct charges at the enemy lines, and victors only if we maneuver behind the city to sack its railways and supply depots. Returning to our major theme, we need to unify the four problems of space and time in a single more fundamental problem from which they can be derived. Those four problems were: 1. Are time and space relational or absolute? 2. Are they smooth or made of chunks? 3. Are they finite or infinite? 4. Are they the same or different? To this I would a fifth question that has concerned me since my own childhood, though it is rarely if ever discussed in philosophy: 5. Why do we always speak only of space and time as a pair, with no third or fourth term ever added? Is "space and time" an adequate topic, or should we replace it with "space, time, and X" or "space, time, X, and Y?" This fifth question may even turn out to be the gateway to the others.

The remainder of this essay gives my imagined posthumous advice to Beatrice and her friends. My strategy is to show how space and time emerge from the structure of objects themselves. This does not ensure agreement with Leibniz against Clarke, since objects themselves are neutral in that dispute. Whether we think of space and time as relational or absolute, in both cases we are concerned with the planets, armies, locusts, and horses that either generate or populate space and time.

3. Objects vs. Accidents, Relations, and Qualities

When the word "object" is mentioned in philosophy, it is generally placed in opposition to the human "subject". This tiresome pair of terms yields an impoverished conception of objects that must be abandoned. The complaint may not sound very original, since thousands of authors not only bemoan a false subject/object divide, but even claim to have overcome it. With hands placed on hearts, they solemnly swear that we cannot have humans without world or world without humans, but only a primordial interdependence of the two. In this way they imagine that they have put an end to the central mistake of modern philosophy. Yet all these thousands of saviors miss the point completely. For even while claiming to surpass the gap between humans and world, they leave this same pair intact at the center of philosophy, even if now as a unified pair. The real problem with subject and object is not the *gap* between them; gaps are bridged easily enough with steel, wood, or humble Elmer's glue. Instead, the real problem is that human and world are taken as the two fundamental ingredients that must be found in any situation. As a result, the relation between humans and apples is assumed to be philosophically more significant than the relations between apples and trees, apples and sunlight, or apples and wind. These inanimate rapports are generally tossed aside to the natural sciences, while philosophy restricts itself to narrow meditation on a pampered twofold of people and things. The vast majority of present-day philosophy still inhabits this same parochial rift, mistaking it for the universe as a whole. It hardly matters whether the gap is preserved (Kant) or purportedly overcome (phenomenology). The point is that no other rifts are taken into account. Yet the heartrending duel or marriage between object and subject is not fundamental. Far deeper is the triple interplay between an object and its accidents, relations, and qualities. Since the new approach to space and time hinges on the precise character of these three tensions, I will now summarize them briefly.

The term "object" will be used in the broadest possible sense to designate anything with some sort of unitary reality. "Object" can refer to trees, atoms, and songs, and also to armies, banks, sports franchises, and fictional characters. Some objects may be real in the usual sense of external physical existence, but others may not. Donald Duck is no less an object than a pillar of granite. This entails that, while "object" has certain similarities to the classical term "substance", there are important differences as well. Many past philosophers defined substance as the smallest, the simplest, the most eternal, the most natural, or the most real thing in the world. Object-oriented philosophy abandons such obsolete criteria from the start. I hereby bequeath the following brief rules about objects to my ambitious crew of five-year-old disciples:

1. Relative size does not matter: an atom is no more an object than a skyscraper.

2. Simplicity does not matter: an electron is no more an object than a piano.

3. Durability does not matter: a soul is no more an object than cotton candy.

4. Naturalness does not matter: helium is no more an object than plutonium.

5. Reality does not matter: mountains are no more objects than hallucinated mountains.

What makes something an object is not any of the features just discarded, but the simple fact that something is or seems to be *one* thing. This brings us back to the basic tension between an object and its accidents, relations, and qualities. Consider the table at which I type these words. Although fairly clean, the table is covered with streaks of dirt, and reflects the dim sunlight of a January afternoon in Amsterdam. A few hours from now, the table will have been cleaned and the sun will have vanished, giving the table an entirely different appearance. When that happens, will I say that the table is not the same table? Of course not. I will merely say that certain accidental features of the table have changed. The table is something deeper than its transient, shifting facade.

Now consider as well the position of the table with respect to other entities in the world. The table is a specific distance from the door, and also a specific distance from both Rotterdam and Shanghai. For most of its lifespan the table belonged to a world where Benazir Bhutto, Sir Edmund Hillary, and Bobby Fischer were living agents; indeed, they might have sat at this table themselves had they chosen to visit. But with the recent deaths of these celebrities, the table now stands in different relations to the rest of the world, however irrelevant this fact may be to its function as a table. When I move the table slightly, or when Bhutto dies at the hands of assassins, do I say that the table is no longer the same thing, merely because its network of involvements has changed? Nonsense. I will say that the table is the same table, but has entered into different relations with the rest of the world. The table is no longer one at which the dead celebrities can sit, but this hardly affects its innermost reality.

Now let's consider the inherent qualities of the table. Here I speak not of the accidental streaks of dirt or the random amount of sunlight in which it bathes at any moment. Instead, I refer to the qualities of the table that it needs in order to be precisely that table: something like its *essential* qualities, whatever those may be. There are certain traits that the table could not lose without being something else altogether. We may be wrong about which qualities are essential, or may disagree about them, but that is a separate problem. What is interesting here is that this situation is not the same as the first two. While we seem to be able to change the accidents and relations of a thing without changing the thing itself, this is untrue of the qualities, since by definition these are the ones that characterize it intimately. But if we cannot change a thing's qualities without changing the thing, this still does not entail that they are one and the same. It is conceivable, after all, that different objects might share some or most of their qualities. It also seems that objects cannot just be lists of assorted qualities, but must have an organizing principle linking them together in a specific way: even a "bundle of qualities" needs a bundling medium. This third opposition is certainly trickier and more elusive than the others. But we can at least say that there is reasonable doubt as to whether an object can be regarded as just a fusion of loosely assembled qualities.

Admittedly, no proof has been given of these three oppositions so far. I have merely adopted an almost commonsense view that objects are different from their accidents, relations, and qualities. This is not to say that common sense amounts to a proof: common sense believes in many stupid things, and at times we pay a heavy price for following it. Furthermore, it is not hard to find philosophies that deny the very existence of the three oppositions just described. For instance, Alfred North Whitehead and Bruno Latour do not distinguish between an entity and its accidents or relations, since both thinkers view an object as utterly concrete in all respects, not as some internal diamond encrusted with an accidental grime of relations. Meanwhile, for David Hume and other empiricists, an object is a bundle of qualities and nothing more. My claim is that common sense is right on these matters while these celebrated philosophers are wrong. An object is no seamless fusion, but is fatally torn between itself and its accidents, relations, and qualities: a set of tensions that makes everything in the universe possible, including space and time. To map these rifts more closely is the mission of object-oriented philosophy, a task that will largely be left to the future school of Beatrice and her friends. For my time on earth is nearly finished.

4. Two Kinds of Objects

To build on the greatness of others is to build on rock, however modest our own talents. I nominate phenomenology as the philosophical bedrock of the twentieth century. This is not to suggest that this school is without flaws, or that its current proponents correctly grasp its key insights, but only that Husserl and Heidegger both belong on the shortest list of recent philosophers who have made decisive breakthroughs. My claim is that both the friends and enemies of phenomenology are too occupied with peripheral features of Husserl and Heidegger and thereby miss the point. Phenomenology is above all an *object-oriented* school whose major treasures are still overlooked. Husserl builds his philosophy on intentional objects, while Heidegger builds his on the veiled real objects known as tools, or later "things". The fact that Heidegger reserves the term "object" for pejorative use is irrelevant, since he clearly brushes against our topic under a different name. Only by crosbreeding the objects of Husserl with those of Heidegger do we obtain the elements of a new philosophy of objects, and hence of space and time.

Husserl's phenomenology is best understood as an effort to fortify philosophy against the encroachments of natural science. For Husserl all physical explanations of color or sound are derivative, since these infer causal mechanisms that are never directly given to us. What is directly given is my own unreflective experience. In everyday life I smell bread and hear the rushing of trains. These experiences lie prior to any interaction of chemicals or sonic waves with my nervous system, since these remain only a theory. In short, philosophy should *bracket* the outer world, suspending judgment on what happens outside our own experience, and focus on a pure description of what is given. Now that we have described human experience as the foundation for all other realities, we seem to have reached a form of idealism. But it is here that both critics and admirers of Husserl have strayed from the path. The critics see Husserl as just another idealist, and not a very original one. I have often heard Husserl described as "a less interesting version of Descartes" or "a less interesting version of Kant". Let's ignore for the moment any possible disputes as to whether Descartes and Kant were really idealists. The more interesting question is whether phenomenology is just a recycled version of previous idealisms.

The answer is no. Too much attention is paid to Husserl's bracketing of the real world, and too little attention to what results from that bracketing. Everyone knows the proverbial tale of Husserl's semester in Freiburg describing a mailbox. While such concrete descriptions are admittedly scarce in Husserl, they are found by the truckload in many of his heirs: especially Merleau-Ponty, Levinas, and Lingis. These later figures actually deliver what Husserl had already promised: a concrete description of specific objects such as food, labor camps, black pens, parrots, and flowers. Now, it is strikingly difficult to find such descriptions of tangible objects in those former idealists who are supposedly plagiarized by a supposedly unoriginal Husserl, who is wrongly accused of rehashing the insights of Descartes and Kant. The reason that concrete description is possible in phenomenology is because Husserl is a philosopher of intentional *objects*. True enough, he must bracket the existence of the black pen in any outer physical world. And granted, he is forced to ignore any difference between the mailbox as solid physical object and as paranoid fantasy. But even though an intentional object is bracketed, it is not *only* bracketed. There is a good reason why Husserl's idealism has such a strangely realist flavor. This reason lies in the stubborn tenacity of the intentional object, which forever resists the machinations of the ego or absolute knowing. The most important aspect of intentional objects is that they are something different from the profiles through which they become manifest; the mailbox is something more, or perhaps something less, than any of its specific incarnations in perception. With this step, Husserl opposes the entire tradition of empiricism, which views objects as nothing over and above a bundle of palpable qualities.

Recall that for Husserl, we can circle the mailbox from various angles and distances, viewing it amidst different emotions at different times of day, and can even have it repainted or strung with ornaments. Within certain limits, none of these modifications of the mailbox make us think that we are seeing a different thing. Instead, the mailbox endures as one object for us, even as its apparent qualities shift wildly. This cuts against the grain of the empiricist school, which mocks the supposed object as an empty *je ne sais quoi* blindly posited to explain why certain palpable qualities of color or texture often seem mutually attached. Husserl reverses this empiricist doctrine in the little-read *Logical Investigations* II by subordinating qualities to objects. We do not experience red, shiny, cold, slippery, and sweet, then arbitrarily fuse such genuine qualities into fictitious union, as Hume believes. Rather, we experience the qualities as if they emanated from an underlying object. For Merleau-Ponty, the red of an apple and the red of blood are not the same color even if their wavelengths of reflected light are found to be absolutely identical. What comes first are not qualities, but intentional or ideal objects. If there is a true "permanent tension" in Husserl's philosophy, it does not lie between a bracketed physical world and an immanent phenomenal one, since the former plays little to no role in his thinking. The real tension for Husserl lies *within* the immanent realm, between intentional objects and the qualities that emanate from them. No such tension can be found in previous idealisms. To miss this difference is to betray a certain tone-deafness to phenomenology's new music. Husserl's lasting contribution stems from his exploration of intentional objects. Even those who proclaim him an idealist (as I myself do) cannot deny that his world is populated with objects. Though they are not real physical objects able to break and burn their neighbors, they remain objects of a different sort.

This brings us to a parallel error made by Husserl's admirers, who mostly deny that he is an idealist at all. For these mainstream phenomenologists, the intentionality of consciousness is already enough to overcome the subject-object divide. After all, consciousness is always conscious *of* something. To gaze upon a black pen supposedly takes me beyond myself, placing me in a rich world of relational interplay with the things themselves. The problem with this line of argument is clear enough. Once the bracketing of the world occurs, we have lost any reality apart from how it is announced to us. The black pens, pine cones, mailboxes, and burning churches described by phenomenologists are purely immanent objects, whether or not they are figments of a deluded mind. And even in those cases where the intentional objects do correspond to something in reality, the mailbox described in my consciousness is not a mailbox buffeted by real wind and protecting real packages from real snow. There is only one name for what results from Husserl's bracketing method, and that name is idealism. Another name for intentionality is *"immanent* objectivity", and there is no such thing as "realism of immanence", "internal realism", or "things-themselves-for-us", however popular these notions may have become. If any philosophy does not allow two non-human objects to affect each other even when humans are not looking, there is no honest way to avoid calling that philosophy idealist.

All of this can be summarized as follows. Husserl's admirers and opponents both miss the point by failing to put intentional objects at the center of consideration. For Husserl's enemies he is a mere idealist, though in fact there is nothing "mere" about this idealism, whose object-oriented structure is as foreign to Hegel and Fichte as it would be to the great mystics of the Ganges. For his fans, our relation to intentional objects is supposedly enough to escape from idealism, although no such escape has occurred. We could put the matter more charitably by saying that the pro- and anti-Husserl factions are both half-right. His critics are right that he is an idealist, and his friends are right that he directs us toward objects. But his critics think this means "idealism without objects", while his friends think it means "objects without idealism". What both sides fail to see is that an *object-oriented idealism* is possible: and not just possible, since Husserl's philosophy is precisely this. What makes trees, stars, windmills, centaurs, and warlocks equally intentional objects is that all withstand numerous modifications of the profiles by which they are manifest. So much for the theme of intentional objects.

An altogether different sort of object emerges from the works of Heidegger. In the famous tool-analysis, Heidegger observes that our usual way of dealing with entities is not theoretically gazing upon them, but simply relying on them. Tool-beings recede into a silent background as our conscious awareness is occupied elsewhere. While typing this article I focus on the computer screen and on the thoughts at the forefront of my mind. Yet I also rely on the keyboard that is barely noticed, the inner circuitry of the computer, the English grammar that is now almost automatic for me, and the brain and blood cells that enable me to function as a unified living being. Let's call these entities *real* objects as opposed to intentional ones, since they are not the same as the objects described by Husserl. First, Husserl's objects are forbidden any potency in the real world, while Heidegger's tools clearly have it: if any of these silent entities (such as keyboard, grammar, or brain cells) were to fail, there would be consequences fatal to this article or even to its author. Second, while Heidegger's tools withdraw into darkness, Husserl's objects are always there before us from the start. It is true that we never see all the qualities of a Husserlian apple simultaneously. Yet the apple as a whole is there from the outset, an imperious unit to which the numerous apple-qualities are enslaved. We look straight through whatever qualities are currently accessible, right to the apple as a whole. This makes the intentional apple entirely different from an apple in its secluded reality, which hides to such a degree that we can only hint at it.

The most common interpretation of Heidegger's tool-analysis is a pragmatist sort of reading: all conscious theory emerges from a previous unconscious practice. In this way, Husserl's phenomenology of appearances would merely be subordinated to Heidegger's hermeneutic phenomenology; since everything emerges from a shadowy background, we can only interpret objects rather than accessing them lucidly. This is fair enough, as far as it goes, yet it completely misses the real challenge posed by Heidegger's tools. We can start by agreeing that any explicit theory of a thing, or any perception of it, will oversimplify that thing. To look at apples or to develop a theory of apples means to reduce them to a caricature of their shadowy depth, which

only insofar as someone is sincerely dealing with it. If I close my eyes and fall asleep, the intentional apple has vanished. But even as I sleep and dream, the real apple (assuming I was not just hallucinating) continues to unleash its force on all objects in the vicinity.

5. Emanation and Occasional Cause

But if the real apple unleashes force in this way, it remains puzzling how it can do so. The point of real objects is that they withdraw absolutely from all relation, and hence from all contact of any sort. We might speak of a partial unveiling of the apple, a sort of asymptotic approach to the apple-in-itself. But any "partial" visibility of the apple will already be quite different from the apple in its own right, which labors silently in invisible depths. This makes relationality a major philosophical problem. It no longer seems evident how one thing is able to interact with another, since each thing in the universe seems to withdraw into a private bubble, with no possible link between one and the next. The same problem arose for different reasons in the tradition of occasionalist philosophy. For occasionalists from medieval Iraq onwards, created substances could not be granted the power of interaction under pain of blasphemy, and hence God was needed to mediate between any two things that might interact. The major flaw with this solution is that it arbitrarily grants one superior entity, God, a relational power withheld from all others. It thereby dodges the question of how this occurs, hiding behind the curtain of the True Faith. Even so, the problem with objects that we now face is the same as this admirable occasionalist problem. Since experience has taught me that it is difficult to free the term "occcasional cause" from theological overtones, I have coined the phrase "vicarious causation" to replace it. The point of vicarious causation is that we should not select one super-entity to be given a magical power to touch other things as long as other entities are denied the same power. Instead, we must find some way to build the capacity for vicarious causation into the structure of every entity that exists. That is not the task of the present article. Here I only wish to emphasize that the real entity lies at an absolute distance from its phenomenal appearance to some other entity.

The situation is quite different when it comes to the intentional objects described by Husserl. These do not withdraw in the least, and for two separate reasons. On the one hand, they do not veil themselves from me. While it is true that I can never see all sides or angles of a house simultaneously, it is not the case that the intentional house is hidden from view. True, the real house itself always recedes from any contact with me or anything else. But the same is not true for the phenomenal house of consciousness, even though it is never fully incarnate with all possible attributes from all possible viewpoints at once. For the house is already present before me as soon as I begin to explore it. My explorations are explorations *of the house*, at least until I decide that I have been misidentifying the object and am actually seeing something else. So, intentional or phenomenal objects are immediately present for me as soon as I merely take them seriously. Second, there is never just one intentional object in my consciousness, but many. I do not see a tree without also perceiving the surrounding grass, clouds, wolves, drumbeats, and odors. Intentional objects are characterized by *contiguity*. In this sense, intentional objects also do not fully recede from one another, for they are assembled together simultaneously for a viewer.

But an all-important proviso must be added, though there is no time to develop it here. We have distinguished between real objects and intentional ones. And intentional objects are normally regarded as mental, and are usually even restricted to the human. Thus, the encounter with intentional objects might be regarded as a sort of first-person psychological experience. But in fact, intentional objects are far more rudimentary than objects of conscious experience. Although all our examples of intentional objects so far have come from the sphere of human consciousness, this is by no means necessary. We have not yet claimed to know what consciousness is, nor do we need to do so in order to illuminate what intentionality is. Recall that intentionality has two basic features. First, it is occupied with intentional objects. Second, those objects are surrounded by a cloud of accidents that can be varied infinitely without change to the intentional objects themselves. Now note, somewhat surprisingly, that both features hold even in the case of contact between inanimate objects. If we imagine one billiard ball striking another, we need not adopt a panpsychist theory of conscious plastic balls. Yet one ball still must encounter the other *as an object*. Otherwise it could not be a barrier of any sort, and would pass straight through it, unaffected. (The option that the ball could encounter disembodied qualities has already been discounted.) Yet by definition it cannot encounter the real ball, but only an intentional image of it. Meanwhile, it must also encounter that ball in some specific configuration of accidents: say, at a particular temperature, even though within certain limits the fluctuation of that temperature makes no difference to the ball as a ball. The case can be argued at greater length elsewhere, but the conclusion will be as follows: intentional objects do not belong solely to the precious mental sphere of humans, but to any interaction between any two things whatsoever. Instead of calling them intentional objects, let's call them simply "images" or "simulacra", in less bulky and less psychologically burdened terminology.

We must now take one additional strange step. Husserl had noted the paradox that intentionality is both singular and plural. For on the one hand, the relation between the perceiver and a chair is *one*: it is a single relation that can be analyzed retrospectively by a later moment of consciousness, or even by another person who observes and describes it. This makes the relation an *object* in our broad sense of the term; it has a unified reality that no external observation can ever exhaust. But at the same time intentionality is also multiple, and for obvious reasons. If I fused together fully with all the chairs and candles that I perceived, there would be a single unified phenomenon without two separate terms. I would not be taking something seriously that lies outside me, since I would have fused directly into that thing. The weird implication is that the candle and I are two separate entities inhabiting the interior of a larger entity that contains us both: namely, the relation that unifies us. An entire philosophy will unfold from this proposition. But the current article is focused on space and time, and hence we can sidestep this additional theme. All that needs to be said here is as follows. The world consists of only two elements: objects and their interiors. Those interiors are speckled with intentional objects, which we have also called images or simulacra. But we have also seen that objects never touch, since they recede into the monastic solitude of private vacuums. But on the interior of objects, something does happen. This is a place where one object (a human observer, for instance) is sincerely occupied with images, and where various images crowd side by side, each of them encrusted with countless accidents. More deserves to be said about these issues, but no more is needed to return to the topic of space and time.

We began by saying that object-oriented philosophy distinguishes between an object and its accidents, qualities, and relations. The difference between object and accident has been seen to play out in the realm of intentional objects: accidents exist only for a perceiver of intentional objects, whether that perceiver be living or inanimate. No river, windmill, donkey, or clown that we encounter is confronted in the naked purity of its essence. Each of them reflects transient light and appears to mirror some fleeting mood, which are unimportant since all can be varied without changing what the thing seems to be. We have spoken of how the specific profiles of a thing at any moment (the house from such-and-such an angle and distance) seem to *emanate* from that thing. This echo of Neoplatonic terminology is deliberate. But against the Neoplatonic doctrine that emanation yields a product less real and less good than that from which it hails, the surface of colors and smells emanates from an intentional object that is somehow *less* than its various incarnations, since we can subtract these encrustations while leaving the thing unchanged. Here we have a first site of emanation, with one kind of reality apparently emitted by another. It is a horizontal emanation within the sensual realm; its tension is the very stuff of human perception, though not just of human perception. But there is also a second emanation, a vertical one. We have seen that a real object withdraws from all its relations, remaining deeper than they are, unexhausted by them. Yet there is also an attachment between the concealed subterranean tree and its image for some other object, such as a human. In both cases, there is a tension between an object and that through which it is announced. We might say that a city skyline emanates (or "expresses", as DeLanda would say) the specific accidental profiles by which we recognize it at any moment. In a different sense, we could say that a real hammer emanates the hammer-images through which it is encountered. The first is an emanation from intentional objects to accidents, and the second an emanation from real objects into the intentional realm.

We now come to the central claim of this article: the emanation of accidents from an intentional object *is time*, and the emanation of intentional objects from real ones *is space*. Space and time are neither empty containers (Clarke) nor produced by relations between objects (Leibniz), but something diverted slightly from the Leibnizian position. Let's begin with space. It would be mistaken to follow Leibniz literally and say that space is simply generated by the relations between things. For it is just as true that space is the site of *non*-relation between things. If space were simply made up of relations, we would have a systematic gridwork with each object utterly defined by its relations with all the others, and the universe would become a single lump interrelated to the point of homogeneity. Such a lump provides no room for anything like space, which by definition would contain only one position: that of the lump as a whole. Any attempt to describe space adequately must concede that space involves the relation of objects that do not *entirely* relate. In other words, the simultaneous withdrawal of real objects from one another and their partial contact through simulacra is space itself. This network of objects is not made possible by space, nor is it the "condition of possibility" of space. Rather, space itself *is* the mutual exteriority of objects, and their partial contact with images of one another, however this might occur. Then space is not relations, but the *tension* between objects and their relations. If Leibniz had refused to identify the monad with its perceptions, he would have arrived at the position now being defended.

Likewise, the emanation that strings intentional objects together with their accidents is nothing other than time. It should be noted that two distinct aspects of time are often mixed together. On the one hand, there is time imagined as a series of moments stretching out one after the other, and Bergson is right to identify this form of "time" with space, while Minkowski and Einstein are apparently just as right (as far as we know) to collapse this form of time into a wider four-dimensional space-time. These issues of physics need not concern us here. The relevant form of time for us is found in the sensation of time passing. It is the sensation of a continuum, not of a series of discrete poses in the manner of claymation films. If I stare at a tree as the light and odors swirl wildly around it, with the tree nonetheless remaining the same for me, we have a clear example of the experience of time. Since this merely involves the swirling of accidental surface features, we can see that time itself changes nothing. Nor is there any reason to speculate about time travel, since time has no "arrow" at all. Time, in the sense of this article, reverses back and forth wildly while changing nothing in the least: by definition, time is purely accidental. To speak of wishing to travel in time back to 1989 is merely to speak of wishing that we could return to the system of objects that we recall as having been in force during that year. But many of those objects have been destroyed, and this is irreversible. The reason for its irreversibility is that two objects uniting to give rise to a third does not necessarily entail that the third can decompose into its parents. The asymmetry comes not from time (which is perfectly symmetrical) but from objects themselves.

Stated differently, space is the mutual externality of partially linked objects, while time is the interior of objects themselves. Time is the emanation of accidents from intentional objects, while space is the emanation of images from real ones. The difference between objects and accidents gives us time, while the difference between objects and relations gives us space. Since we have said that two objects can relate only on the interior of a third, it follows that there are infinitely many times, each unfolding on the interior of some vacuum-like space. Here too we find the materials for an entire philosophy.

But the alert reader will have wondered what happened to our third distinction, between objects and their inherent qualities apart from any relational contact with that thing. These inherent qualities can also be described as *essential* qualities. Millions of people are united these days in a shared contempt for essence, yet this contempt cannot be defended. Once we accept that an object exceeds all possible relations to it, we know that it has independent reality. And once it has such reality, it must have it as a *specific* reality, or all objects would be alike. Hence there is no avoiding a concept of essence. Yet this does not entail any of the dangers normally associated with essence. There is no need for us to say that essences are eternal, that they are unchangeable, that they trap humans into rigid social roles defined by nature, that they are natural kinds created by God, that human knowledge can adequately capture them, or even that some humans (such as Germans, Greeks, white males, and philosophers) more closely approximate the human essence than others (such as Romans, Jews, non-white females, and factory workers). To defend essence is not to conspire in a sinister plot by the Party of Reaction. It is nothing more than to insist that objects are not exhausted by their relations to other objects. To take the opposite approach requires that one adopt a radical metaphysics of relation in the manner of Whitehead and Latour, as rejected above.

At any rate, the tension between an object and its qualtities is also a form of emanation. Here too the essential qualities seem to belong to the object, yet are not identical with it, even though it requires them. And this means that our fifth question about space and time has already been answered. Space and time no longer stand alone. They are usually treated as the unique king and queen of the cosmos, without rival, even if one is normally considered in three dimensions and the other is not. But by approaching space and time from the direction of objects, we have managed to redefine them as emanations from objects. This pinpoints an empty space on our map where a third emanation should be found: just as good physics foresees the existence of unknown particle families, or as Mendeleev's table predicted chemical elements not yet found. The third emanation that accompanies time (objects vs. accidents) and space (objects vs. relations), is the emanative tension between an object and its qualities. It is not surprising that we have no direct access to this tension as we do to time and space, since by nature essence unfolds only within a shadowy underworld with which no direct contact is possible. As we have seen, the traditional name for the tension between a thing and its qualities is *essence*. Instead of speaking of philosophies of space and time, we must now speak of space, time, and essence as a trio of interrelated terms. Earlier I cited five traditional questions about time and space. The object-oriented approach has already enabled us to stumble across an answer to the fifth question, the dearest one to me since childhood. Namely, space and time do not deserve to be treated alone, since the problem of essence belongs on the same footing as these two. Whether there is a fourth emanation, a missing retroactive one between intentional objects and *real* qualities, is a trickier question best left for another occasion.[60] But once space and time were redefined as emanations, it became clear that essence belongs on the same footing as these two— just as qualities belong on the same footing as accidents and relations. In each of these cases we are dealing with a reality that is somehow attached to objects though not identical with them. Now, we might wonder if object-oriented philosophy can shed any light on the other four questions of space and time.

6. Conclusion

The first question was whether space and time are absolute containers without need of content, or whether they are generated solely by the relations between entities. We have already brushed up against a new solution to this question. Time has been described as the tension between an intentional object and its accidents, while space has been defined as the tension between real objects and the distorted way in which they manifest to some other object that encounters them. In fact, the object-oriented model is largely neutral on the famous dispute between Leibniz and Clarke. Space turns out to be generated by the relational (and non-relational) tension between objects, which partly echoes Leibniz. But time unfolds on the inside of infinitely many objects. In this latter sense Clarke and Newton are also supported, with the key difference that there are infinite spatial containers rather than a single giant container identified with the universe as a whole. Each object creates its own internal space, and *ipso facto* its own interior time, laced with duels between images and their accidents.

The second question was whether space and time are continuous or broken into quantized chunks. The object-oriented model suggests that space is broken up into infinite discrete locations whose interaction poses a critical problem. Yet the *internal* life of an object is continuous, filled with a flux of accidents varied through many possible degrees without the underlying intentional objects changing at all. In a certain sense this supports Bergson's tendency to quantize space while avoiding this gesture for time, but without any suggestion that the realm of quanta is an illusion generated by human abstraction. Space itself is quantized, since it is nothing but the relational/nonrelational system of objects, partly linked even as they withdraw into intimate vacuums. And time itself is a continuum, since any time will be filled with enduring pillars (the intentional objects) encrusted with countless permutations of accidents modified within limits to any possible degree of intensity, without change to the images they adorn.

The third question was whether space and time are finite or infinite, a question that Kant declared unanswerable. This question splits into a trio of separate issues: the space part, the time part, and the "unanswerable" part. Let's address these in a slightly different order, proceeding from easiest to most diffcult.

1. "Is time finite or infinite?" Under the object-oriented model time unfolds only on the interior of an object. As long as objects exist, time must exist. The question can thus be rephrased as follows: "must objects always exist?" While the answer to this question is not yet clear, the object-oriented model with its units withstanding surface fluctuation seems to lean toward a certain principle of inertia. An object will not vanish from the universe unless there is a cause for its doing so, and even if an object is destroyed by such a cause, it stands to reason that it would merely split or pulverize it into different residual objects, not into a gaping hole of non-being. If this position can be maintained,

then objects must always exist, and therefore so must time, which is nothing but their inner molten core.

2. "Is the question even answerable?" Kant's agnosticism on these questions is a form of false modesty. For even as he pleads ignorance as to the possible spatio-temporal character of the world itself, he is quite decisive about the phenomenal sphere: all appearance must occur in space and time, as *a priori* forms of pure intuition. This notion does more injustice to space than to time. For the object-oriented model suggests that space is not "intuited" at all, but merely inferred. If time is the tension between an intentional object and its accidents, this emanation unfolds entirely within the sensual sphere, and can be intuited directly. This squares with everyday experience, which does seem to feel time passing, instead of experiencing a stop-action sequence of discrete, statuesque, cinematic poses. The same is not true of space, if space is really the tension between a secluded withdrawn object and its phenomenal image. For the field of our perception might easily be regarded as a two-dimensional hologram; infants seem to treat it that way, reaching for the moon or distant trees as if they were no more distant than a nearby toy. Though it is true that there seems to be a certain "distance" between different regions of my perception, in another sense all parts of my perceptual field are in exactly the same place, since all are present for me right now. But the true concept of spatiality lies in the withdrawal of such objects from my perception, and this can only be inferred, whereas the emanation between intentional objects and their accidents requires no inference, but is felt directly.

More generally, Kant's agnostic method toward the things themselves is annulled by the logic of Heidegger's tool-analysis as presented above. The key step is not so much the veiling of things from human access, which can easily be reconciled with the standard Kantian model. Instead, the key is to realize that no priority can be given to the single rift between human and world, and to realize further that bridging this divide is still no solution. The problem is not the rift, but the fact that the two particular sides of this rift (human and world) are wrongly viewed as fundamental to the fabric of the world. Object-oriented philosophy proclaims that any relation between any two objects automatically produces distortion. This might be a caricature generated by mathematical models of a comet, but it might equally well be the exaggerated form in which the comet and the planet Mars encounter one another. For Kant, cause and effect are defined merely as human categories without validity for things in themselves. But this is a purely arbitrary outlook, one that follows from an equally arbitrary wish to make the human/world relation a very special thing.

3. "Is space finite or infinite?" This question actually pertains to two matters that Kant treated separately. One is young Beatrice's question as to whether the universe goes on forever. The other is the question of whether space breaks down into regions infinitely small or comes to a halt in some final tiny atomic layer that cannot be broken down further. This is the question of possible infinite regress to accompany a possible infinite progress. Both questions are somewhat obscure, but can at least be rephrased in object-oriented terms. Our model does seem to suggest an infinite regress, as preferable both to a finite regress (an atomic theory of reality) and to the option of no regress at all (an idealist theory in which the sole layer of reality is the accessible one). If every object needs an essence in order to be distinct from all others, and every essence is multiple, then every object is likely to have parts, and parts of parts, on down to infinity. But the same infinity does not seem necessary in the other direction. Even if there is good reason to suppose that every object has parts, it does not follow that every object must be a part of some larger object, any more than a child with parents must therefore become a parent itself. It might be the case that the cosmos terminates at its edge in a vast set of childless objects. But

in that case, what would lie outside the cosmos? Nothingness? The answer is unclear.

We now turn to the fascinating fourth question, though little can be said of it here. For Minkowski and Einstein, time and three-dimensional space can be considered as a unified four-dimensional space-time. The object-oriented approach initially dodges this question by treating time as an *experience*, and by treating this experience as an emanation between intentional objects and their accidents, a sphere of reality about which relativity makes no claims at all. Yet the dodge should not be a permanent one. For aassuming that time is truly incommensurable with space in the manner described in this article, philosophy might still wonder why physics has made such great strides by considering them as a four-dimensional continuum.

Some of the ideas in this article have gained credence with the author after years of reflection, while other remain far more puzzling. Yet even these latter ideas serve a purpose. By approaching space and time from a new direction, we elude a number of existing trench wars in philosophy, and will possibly have boosted the morale of Beatrice and her friends at some indefinite future point. The dithering agnosticism of recent philosophy, its obsession with tedious questions of human *access* to the world, can be replaced by a high-rolling metaphysics of objects. The spirit of the archive can be replaced by that of the casino.

10. The Assemblage Theory of Society (2008)

This lecture was given on 8 November, 2008 in Stavanger, Norway. The conference was entitled Deleuze2008: Deleuze in the Open, and was one of several events hosted by Stavanger during its joint reign with Liverpool as one of the 2008 European Capitals of Culture. I was invited to the conference by organizer Arne Fredlund as the replacement for Manuel DeLanda, who was unable to attend. Thus, the most appropriate theme for the paper seemed to be DeLanda himself.

"Assemblage theory" is Manuel DeLanda's most recent name for what he does.[61] It is a theory of society not in the limited sense of human assemblies, but one suggesting that all entities result from a swarm of tinier subcomponents that do not melt into a seamless whole. Assemblage theory is a full-blown ontology; more than this, it is a *good* ontology. Numerous key paradoxes of speculative philosophy arise within minutes once we reflect on the various points of DeLanda's model of the universe, and that is the best sign of a strong philosophical theory. Today I will discuss four central elements of this model: its twofold promotion of realism and assemblages, and its twofold critique of essence and linear causation. Each of these themes has a closely related twin. DeLanda's realism leads him to a theory of *the virtual*; his assemblage theory entails a doctrine of *emergence*; his critique of essence endorses *historical genesis* over fully formed individuals; finally, his critique of linear causation states that certain factors *catalyze* interactions rather than producing them in mechanical fashion. In what follows, I will describe briefly how DeLanda handles all eight of these major themes: realism, the virtual, assemblage, emergence, essence, genesis, causation, and catalysis. The critique of linear causation has immediate implications for the problem of an open universe, the stated theme of this conference.

"Assemblage theory" is the best phrase in DeLanda's writings for tying all these themes together, and assemblages raise new problems with which DeLanda and others must grapple. But the spirit of my remarks will be largely positive, since his books are among my favorite recent works of philosophy. Let's begin with a brief overview of the four major landmarks ahead.

First, DeLanda openly proclaims himself a *realist*. He says this so bluntly and so often that there is no escaping it, however unpopular realism remains even among his fans. While realism has always been a respectable option among analytic philosophers, DeLanda is one of the very few continentally oriented thinkers to declare himself a realist without tortured qualification. Heidegger obviously does not do this, nor do Husserl or Merleau-Ponty. Derrida and Foucault would rather die than call themselves realists, despite Foucault's supposed "materialism". To my knowledge Badiou never describes himself as a realist, nor does Zizek, nor do Deleuze and Guattari. Bruno Latour does make public calls for realism now and then (especially in *Pandora's Hope*), but only at the price of a drastic redefinition of what realism means. If we exclude the younger generation of continental philosophers, only DeLanda can claim to be a realist with a straight face and without ironic tricks. Normally realism is slandered with an unearned adjective, and appears in the form of "naive" realism, a phrase that poses as the name for one type of realism while really insinuating that *all* realism is naive. Whether DeLanda be judged as naive or not, his realism does not resemble the dull commonsense realism of yesteryear. Instead of an arid landscape of solid physical bulks paired with a boring human *cogito* that has the special gift and burden of corresponding with them, DeLanda provides a realism in which realities are never fully actualized even in the physical realm, let alone in our minds. He links this model with Deleuze's "virtual" and uses this term frequently. But it may have even more in common with the "intransitive" realm of Roy Bhaskar, whose influence DeLanda freely admits.

Second, DeLanda holds that every sort of entity is an assemblage. This entails that no object is a seamless whole that fully absorbs its components, and also entails an anti-reductionist model of reality. There is no reason to claim that a quark or electron is more real than Norway, NATO, or the international Deleuze community. There is also no ultimate layer of tiny microparticles to which macro-entities might be reduced. At whatever point we fix our gaze, entities are assembled from other entities: they can be viewed as unified things when seen from the outside, yet they are always pieced together from a vast armada of autonomous components. This also means that Delanda believes in genuine *emergence*. It is not possible to eliminate larger entities by accounting for the behavior of their tiniest physical parts.

Third, DeLanda opposes all forms of essence (and here he parts company with Bhaskar). He objects not only to an otherworldly region of perfect forms, but also to Aristotle's "taxonomic" version of essence, where there are a certain fixed number of natural kinds represented by a number of specific entities; Charles Darwin is the usual rebuttal witness here, and DeLanda summons him as expected. Yet DeLanda also goes a bit further than this, and offers two more pivotal reasons why no individual thing has an essence. One reason is his ultimately Bergsonian vision of entities as historical-genetic processes that cannot be pinned down in specific moments. There is no natural species called hydrogen, but only a vast population of hydrogen atoms, each with its own unique life story beginning in the cores of assorted stars. The other reason is his view, quite prominent in his 2002 Deleuze book but rather faint by 2006, that realities (unlike actualities) belong to a *continuum* rather than being quantized into chunks. This too makes it impossible for any essence to have fixed, distinct outlines, since an essence will necessarily bleed into neighboring possibilities. Today I will reject both of these views, and try to push DeLanda's assemblages in a different direction.

Fourth, while DeLanda surprisingly concedes the existence of old-fashioned linear causation, he thinks it is dwarfed by what he calls catalysis. Cigarettes do not cause cancer in everyone who smokes them, nor do all lung cancer victims smoke cigarettes at some point in life. Hence, the cigarettes must be viewed merely as catalysts for cancer. In DeLanda's eyes, this is already enough to threaten the traditional notion of deterministic causation, which is similar to Bhaskar's argument against determinism. But I will suggest that it merely establishes that linear causes are hard to *know*, without striking at the very fortress of mechanism. I will suggest further that DeLanda needs a much weirder discussion of causal relations, since his anti-actualization views entail anti-relational views, and this in turn makes causation a compelling riddle.

1. Realism

Every thinker uses certain key terms that can be modified or sacrificed when necessary, while others are treated as a matter of life and death. One of DeLanda's life-and-death terms is "realism", rarely a popular word in continental philosophy circles these days. Indeed, the realism/idealism split is often dismissed as a corny pseudo-problem belonging to fossilized olden times. But this is not how DeLanda sees it. In his own words: "there are philosophers who grant reality full autonomy from the human mind…. These philosophers are said to have a *realist ontology*. Deleuze is such a realist philosopher, [which] should distinguish him from most post-modern philosophers which remain basically non-realist."[62] As a reading of Deleuze this might be rejected or simply ignored for any number of reasons, but that is of limited importance here. For as DeLanda puts it: "Readers who feel that the theory developed here is not strictly speaking Deleuze's own are welcome to call it 'neo-assemblage theory', 'assemblage theory 2.0', or some other name."[63]

The important point is that DeLanda identifies postmodern philosophy as "basically non-realist", while taking a frankly realist stance in his own right. For DeLanda "realism" means at the very least that reality has a certain autonomy from the human mind. Thus he makes an initial split between reality as it is, and reality as it appears to the human mind. Human access to reality is a sort of translation, distortion, transformation, simplification, or truncation of it. For DeLanda this holds true even for those parts of reality that *require* human existence. A good example would be human society itself, for as he writes, "though social entities are clearly not mind-independent.... a realist approach to social ontology must assert the autonomy of social entities from the *conceptions* we have of them."[64] To create something does not mean to see through to its depths; we do not drain our children to the dregs by begetting them, but set them loose in the world like wild dogs, beyond our control and often beyond our knowledge.

Yet there is a problem with most forms of realism. The problem is not that realism is "naive" (for would a cynical realism be any better?). Instead, the problem is that realism is often too narrow. Whether we deny things-in-themselves outside the human/world correlate, or insist upon such extra-mental realities, this endless dispute orbits the single dismal pair of human and world. The relation between just these two terms is treated as the magic key that will unlock all the secrets of ontology if solved. One of DeLanda's most important virtues is his avoidance of this claustrophobic human/world duet. For him, realism does not just mean autonomy from the human mind: it means autonomy from any actualization whatsoever, whether or not humans are there to observe it. As opposed to the actual trajectory of actual things through specific points in space-time, DeLanda famously speaks of *singularities* or *attractors*. The actual, discernible behavior of entities is governed by realities that can never be actualized. In DeLanda's words:

> As is well known, the trajectories [in state space] always
> approach an attractor *asymptotically*, that is, they approach it
> *indefinitely close but never reach it*. This means that unlike
> trajectories, which represent the actual states of objects in the
> world, attractors are *never actualized*, since no point of a
> trajectory reaches the attractor itself. It is in this sense that
> singularities represent only the long-term tendencies of a
> system, never its actual states.[65]

These "singularities" seem to be granted a monopoly on the
world's causal power, since DeLanda observes that the actual
behavior of a trajectory "will be determined *not by its previous
states*.... but by the type of the attractor itself".[66] As is well
known, DeLanda describes this status of real attractors as
"virtual", and cites Deleuze from *Difference and Repetition* as
follows:

> The virtual is not opposed to the real but to the actual. *The
> virtual is fully real insofar as it is virtual*.... Indeed, the virtual
> must be defined as strictly a part of the real object— as
> though the object had one part of itself in the virtual into
> which it plunged as though into an objective dimension....
> The reality of the virtual consists of the differential elements
> and relations along with the singular points which corre-
> spond to them. The reality of the virtual is structure. We must
> avoid giving the elements and relations that form a structure
> an actuality which they do not have, and withdrawing from
> them a reality which they do have.[67]

DeLanda cites these words in a spirit of endorsement. But a
certain tension arises that pertains not only to Deleuze or
DeLanda, but to many of the emerging approaches to ontology

that have the greatest popularity today.

The tension is best seen in DeLanda's use of the term "multiplicity", which he presents as the key term of his 2002 book, *Intensive Science and Virtual Philosophy*. After much laying of foundations, he defines a multiplicity as "a nested set of vector fields related to each other by symmetry-breaking bifurcations, together with the distributions of attractors which define each of its embedded levels".[68] There is no need for us to clear up all of the difficult terminology here. We need only focus on the ambivalence in the definition of multiplicity.

For on the one hand, the multiplicity is made up of embedded levels of attractors. And like these "embedded" attractors themselves, the multiplicity as a whole is never actualized. This means that the multiplicity not only exceeds our human awareness of it; instead, it exceeds any actualization whatsoever. Whatever happens to it, whatever comes in contact with it, cannot possibly do it justice. While Bruno Latour claims that an entity is nothing more than what it "modifies, transforms, perturbs, or creates,"[69] such results would be mere actualizations for DeLanda. His attractors, singularities, virtualities, realities, multiplicities would always be something more. If Latour is the ultimate philosopher of relations, for whom a thing has no "accidental" manifestations but is thoroughly bonded to all its specific features here and now, DeLanda is the upside-down Latour: multiplicities are *non-relational*, and robustly remain whatever they are, no matter what their relations may be. This already shows progress beyond the desolate human/world gap or non-gap (it scarcely matters which) because DeLanda's attractors are deeper than their actualization even if no humans are around to witness them. The usual distinction between reality and knowledge of reality is replaced by a more interesting gap between reality and any form of actuality. DeLanda deserves much credit for taking this step.

However, to some extent it remains a two-world theory, at

least in his 2002 book on Deleuze. For him, the actual and the real are two fixed zones operating according to two completely different sets of rules. For as we have already heard him say, the actual behavior of a trajectory "will be determined not by its previous states.... but by the type of the attractor itself."[70] Actual states of affairs are thereby deprived of all causal influence. We are affected by cryptic singularities, not by palpable and measurable actual things. Hidden attractors do all the causal work; definite states of affairs have no impact on succeeding states of affairs or on one another. It follows that the actual world is fragmented into totally discrete districts, each a frivolous ornament encrusting a deeper layer of multiplicities, vector fields, and attractors where reality itself unfolds. But while the various portions of the actual are stripped of all ability to interact, the opposite is strangely true of the real or virtual plane. DeLanda's multiplicities, or "concrete universals" as he calls them, are not only "obscure and distinct" rather than clear and distinct: that is to say, they are not simply withheld from all their divergent actualizations. More than this, they have a tendency to fuse together. As DeLanda puts it, in passing and without explanation: "concrete universals must be thought as meshed together into a continuum. This further blurs the identity of multiplicities, creating zones of indiscernibility where they form a continuous immanent space very different from a reservoir of eternal archetypes."[71]

We find then that DeLanda's *actual* world is made up of sterile nodules unable to affect one another or to relate in any way, while the non-actual zone of reality has no difficulty forming relations at all. There everything bleeds together in a continuum. True enough, DeLanda says that "multiplicities should *not* be considered the capacity to actively interact with one another," and refers to their "neutrality or sterility". He appeals to quasi-causal operators creating "resonances and echoes" between singularities, which "[assure multiplicities] a very special independence" and "[possess] no causal power of their own".[72] Yet DeLanda still speaks of their belonging to a *continuum*, and the fact that it was woven together from initial heterogeneity does not prevent it from being a *single* continuum. His multiplicities are large contraptions somehow relating numerous different attractors and vector fields. And furthermore, he approvingly cites Deleuze's definition of the virtual as a structure of "differential elements and relations." The situation is as follows. For DeLanda, multiplicities exceed all human access, and in fact exceed all actualizations even apart from human awareness. In one sense reality is thoroughly non-relational, since nothing is *fully* actualized. Yet we also read that multiplicities themselves are built of embedded layers of different real components, such as attractors and vector fields. An obvious question to raise is why the relations between real attractors that build up a multiplicity are any less problematic than the relation between the real and the actual, or between two actual things. If no actual trajectory ever does justice to its underlying attractors, it should also be the case that no real multiplicity ever does justice to its own real components. In both cases it is a matter of relations, and relations are simply unable to exhaust their terms.

Stated differently, relations for DeLanda are more problematic in the "vertical" sense that the real cannot be fully deployed or depleted in any actual state of affairs. Despite the discussion of quasi-causes, the supposed *continuum* of multiplicities suggests less of a "horizontal" problem in the virtual realm than in the actual. In other words, the DeLanda of 2002 presents a world in which everything is completely fragmented on top, but subjected to a silky-smooth (though "heterogeneous") blend on the bottom. But even in the 2002 book, this two-layered model of the universe with two different sets of rules is at odds with DeLanda's vivid sense that the world is made up of autonomous, emergent levels. As he states it:

much as between individual cells and the individual organisms which they compose there are several intermediate structures bridging the two scales (tissues, organs, organ systems) so between individual atoms of gold and an individual bulk piece of solid material there are intermediately scaled structures that bridge the micro and macro scales: individual atoms form crystals; individual crystals form small grains; individual small grains form larger grains, and so on. Both crystals and grains of different sizes are individuated following specific causal processes, and the properties of an individual bulk sample emerge from the causal interactions between these intermediate structures.[73]

This is the side of DeLanda's thinking that receives further development in his 2006 book *A New Philosophy of Society*.

The tacit move away from a two-storied house of virtual and actual toward a multi-layered structure of differently scaled assemblies suggests a drift in DeLanda's inspiration from Deleuze toward Roy Bhaskar, founder of the popular Critical Realism movement, and a kindred spirit whose influence DeLanda openly celebrates. If there is one thing DeLanda *dislikes* about Bhaskar, it is his allegiance to the notion of "essence". For reasons soon to be discussed, DeLanda rejects essence altogether. But in other respects DeLanda seems especially close to Bhaskar. In particular, DeLanda's tendency to replace the two-layered structure of real and actual with an endless chain of interlinked forms, each form never fully actualized in its surroundings, seems thoroughly Bhaskarian.

Bhaskar's book *A Realist Theory of Science* was published at the now remote date of 1975, but many of its passages still feel shockingly recent. For instance, there is already a DeLandian flavor to Bhaskar's claim that "real structures exist independently of and are often out of phase with the actual patterns of events".[74] DeLanda openly sides with Bhaskar's critique of "actualism", which is based on "the notion that only the actual (identified as the determinate object of the empirical) is real",[75] and whose most talented recent exponent is surely Bruno Latour. More generally, DeLanda would endorse Bhaskar's concept of "an intransitive dimension [of reality], in which the object is the real structure or mechanism that acts quite independently of [humans] and the conditions which allow [humans] access to it".[76] Bhaskar and DeLanda are also united in not regarding human access to the world as an especially significant ontological event. For Bhaskar the real is independent of actual events, but even these actual events are actual apart from their being empirically perceived by humans: just as real things exist apart from all actualizations, "there could be a world of events without experiences."[77]

Initially there might seem to be disagreement between them over the phrase "flat ontology", since Bhaskar condemns flatness[78] and DeLanda gives it public praise.[79] But on closer inspection they turn out to be using the term in opposite senses, which fully accounts for their different valuations of it. For Bhaskar a flat ontology is one that compresses all of reality into the single plane of empirical givenness to human perception, and therefore is worthy of contempt. For DeLanda, by contrast, a flat ontology is one that allows countless layers of larger and smaller structures to have equal ontological dignity, and hence deserves our endorsement. After all, what these two authors share is not only a belief in a *real* dimension deeper than the actual, but also a view that new "reals" can be created through a process of emergence. Bhaskar does not view reductionism any more favorably than DeLanda. In Bhaskar's own words:

> the fact that the properties of everyday objects, at what has been picturesquely described [by Wilfrid Sellars] as the zone of the middle dimensions, can be explained in terms of the very small (or very large) does not render them less real than

the entities that account for them; anymore than zinc and sulphuric acid cease to react in a certain way when we explain their reaction in terms of the atomic structure.[80]

This passage is as a forerunner of DeLanda's attack on both micro- and macro-reductionism, which seek to reduce entities either to their tinier components or to their wider social context. Against such attempts, Bhaskar insists that "if black bodies are real, then so are physicists, if charged particles are real then so are thunderstorms. In short, emergence is an irreducible feature of our world, i.e. it has an irreducibly ontological character."[81] The process that leads smaller levels to build up into larger ones *"has to be understood in terms of causal connections*, not correspondence rules".[82] That is to say, "zinc" is not a loose human nickname for what is really just a tiny swarm of quarks and electrons or infinitesimal strings, but refers to a newly emergent and dignified autonomous reality called zinc. Bhaskar goes so far as to suggest that we will never reach any terminal point of tiniest possible things without parts, since he "can see no reason for supposing" that "the stratification of the world has.... entities that are truly ultimate."[83]

What we have in Bhaskar, as in most of DeLanda's writings, is a vision of the world as a chain of ascending and descending compounds, each of them autonomous from the pieces that create them and equally independent of the wider contexts in which they are enmeshed. A pencil is irreducible to atoms, but is also irreducible to the society that produced it *and* to the full range of pencil-effects that it generates. Functionialism proves to be as great a danger to emergence as reductionism. Philosophy cannot ignore "the picturesque zone of the middle dimensions", because that is what objects or multiplicities are. What we have in Bhaskar and in the DeLanda of 2006 is a multi-layered rather than two-layered model of the world. Bhaskar's universe is utterly quantized. It is broken into jumpy chunks, each of them generated by real causal work below. Put differently, DeLanda in 2002 asserts a continuum of multiplicities, a single "real" layer shared equally by all that is real. For Bhaskar by contrast, and for DeLanda '06 (and already in the cited passage on gold in 2002) each emergent entity creates a new "real" at its own scale, and each of these reals belongs only to the entity in question rather than being partly shared in a continuum with all other things. Bhaskar's "intransitive" reality is just as chunky or quantized as his "transitive" actuality. Attractors are just as hermetically sealed from one another as actual sticks and stones. As Bhaskar colorfully puts it, in denouncing Antony Flew's deplorable claim that "God makes the spectrum and man makes the pigeonholes,"[84]

> I can find no possible warrant for such an assumption. Taken literally, it would imply that a chromosome count is irrelevant in determining the biological sex of an individual, that the class of the living is only conventionally divided from the class of the dead, that the chemical elements reveal a continuous gradation in their properties, that tulips merge into rhododendron bushes and solid objects fade gaseously away into empty space.[85]

When DeLanda begins to speak in 2006 of assemblages rather than multiplicities, this might seem like nothing more than a minor terminological shift. But the continuum of multiplicities capable of easy mutual contact disappears in favor of a Bhaskarian world of unactualized real chunks of every shape and size. This yields numerous philosophical rewards, but gives rise to unaddressed problems as well.

2. Assemblage

We have seen that DeLanda rejects any absolute distinction between "micro" and "macro" levels of explanation. An entity is always "macro" when compared to its tinier components, but always "micro" when compared into those larger assemblages in which it might participate. In this sense, all entities are picturesque intermediate zones, positioned somewhere in a chain of ascending and descending assemblages that are partially but not totally interlinked. An assemblage is "not.... a seamless whole,"[86] but neither is it "a mere aggregate.... without properties that are more than the sum of its parts."[87] And to repeat, if DeLanda's ontology is "flat", this is not the flatness of a single immanent plane where all is continuum. In some respects it is more like the flat ontology of Latour (a thinker with whom he otherwise has little in common) through its placing of all tiny and gigantic assemblages on the same footing. It is true that DeLanda does not reject immanence in favor of some other-worldly dimension; he is the earthliest thinker one can imagine. But just like Bhaskar, DeLanda *is* a philosopher of the much-maligned "deep and hidden". Assemblages are transfactual, or to coin a new term, they are trans*actual*. They are never fully actualized. In fact, they cannot even be *partly* actualized, given DeLanda's view that even a motionless object still fluctuates faintly around an attractor rather than sitting directly on top of it. For DeLanda and Bhaskar, the deep and hidden is speckled throughout every layer of our universe, and is not to be found merely in some dank Heideggerian spring at the bottom of the world.

But the key point was as follows: instead of an accessible layer of the world where everything is fully actualized and fully powerless vis-à-vis other actualities, and a deeper unactualized layer of continuum, we find a duality at each and every layer of the world. We no longer have a fully determinate "actual" dog cut off from all other entities, shadowed by a pre-individual pre-dog that only becomes individualized through its relations with other things. It is not as though individual objects were always actual, and the real made up entirely of pre-individuals. Instead, individual entities have a non-actualized reality, and it belongs to each entity alone, not to a continuum prior to all autonomous things.

For all the appeal of the term "assemblage", we must remember how one-sided it is. The concept of assemblage has useful polemical value when dealing with old-fashioned, natural, unified substances; we can oppose these petrified ancient units by saying that entities do not occur as unified natural kinds, but are composed of mighty armadas of tiny subcomponents. This is one side of the story, and a good side. But recall that an assemblage is never fully actualized: a machine or a human society not only exceeds our conception of it, but must also exceed any actualization of it. That is to say, it must exceed any relational effect that it has on other portions of the world, given its independence from any particular effects it might have in the world at large. This is the ambivalence described earlier: although an assemblage is formed from components in relation, it is an emergence that exceeds those components. And along with exceeding the reality of its parts, it is also deeper than any outer effects it might have, and might not have any effects at all while still retaining its reality. It is far from clear, for instance, that electoral coalitions exist only in the moment of their fabrication. There may have been several real "McCain victory coalitions" that simply went untapped by bumbling strategists. In similar fashion, a certain new musical style of world-historic genius might be heard on the Stavanger waterfront this evening, yet still go unnoticed by recording companies, journalists, or even the musicians themselves.

After all, this lies at the heart of DeLanda's thinking: along with being an assemblage, an entity is also an *emergence*. If we merely gloat over the pluralistic overtones of the word "assemblage", if we sneer at the reactionary dupes who naively believe in real unities and prove our cutting-edge credentials by decomposing all unities into clusters, aggregates, or bundles, we miss half of DeLanda's point. For an entity *emerges*; it is something more than all clusters and aggregates, and is no bundle of properties glued together through the habit of customary conjunction. Entities or objects (I will use such names for emergent assemblages) are not just social creatures generated by assemblies and entering into new ones. By the same stroke, they are also *cut off* from these societies. They withhold themselves from their relations with the outer world insofar as they are never fully actualized, and withhold themselves from their own pieces by exceeding those parts and forming a new reality. They are autonomous. In the terminology of computer science, they are "encapsulated". In the former case we find that they are irreducible to functions, and in the latter that they are irreducible to pieces. But to push the point further, we ought to look at DeLanda's own criteria for emergence. Though he does not pretend to be their originator, he does give a more interesting list than usual. He does not list these features in an actual table, but they are developed from roughly pages 34-40 of *A New Philosophy of Society*:

*Criterion One: an assemblage tends to have retroactive effects on its parts. He credits Bhaskar with this point. In DeLanda's own words: "although a whole emerges from the interactions among its parts, once it comes into existence it can affect those parts.... In other words.... we need to elucidate.... the macro-micro mechanisms through which a whole provides its component parts with *constraints and resources* placing limitations on what they can do while enabling novel performances."[88]

*Criterion Two: an assemblage may be characterized by "redundant causation." This second feature of assemblages turns out to create certain tensions for DeLanda's thought, as will be seen shortly. The basic idea is that the same emergent assemblage might have arisen from any number of different processes, rendering the exact details of its history irrelevant. By way of example, he says that "we may be justified in explaining [an] emerging coalition as a the result of the interaction between entire [large-scale] communities if an explanation of the micro-details [of individual discussions] is unnecessary because several micro-causes would have led to a similar outcome."[89]

*Criterion Three: causal power. Obviously an emergent assemblage might have causal effects on entities *other* than its own parts as well. As he tells us, "social assemblages larger than individual persons have objective existence because.... they can causally affect other assemblages at their own scale. The fact that in order to exercise their causal capacities, internally as well as externally, these [larger] assemblages use people as a medium of interaction does not compromise their autonomy any more than the fact that people must use some of their bodily parts.... compromises their own relative autonomy from their anatomical components."[90]

*Criterion Four: the ability to generate *new* parts. Here DeLanda notes that "while some parts must pre-exist the whole, others may be generated by the maintenance processes of an already existing whole: while cities are composed of populations of inter-personal networks and organizations, it is simply not the case that these populations had to be there prior to the emergence of a city. In fact, most networks and organizations come into being as parts of already existing cities."[91]

Other criteria might be dreamed up. For instance, it seems that the existing list is too focused on the relation between the assemblage and its parts rather than the assemblage and the larger world. But a more important problem is that the list seems focused on what an assemblage *does* rather than what it *is*. That is to say, it seems too focused on what an assemblage "modifies, transforms, perturbs, or creates," Latour's formula for a pragmatist criterion for reality rather than a strictly DeLandian realist one. As we have already seen, the non-actualized autonomy of entities implies that real entities might exist that have no effect at all: as with attractors for which no entity ever happens to enter its basin of attraction.

In other words, three of the four items listed above are all environmental *symptoms* of a new assemblage rather than features of the assemblage itself. To say that an entity is nothing more than its retroactive effects on its own parts, its production of new parts, or its causal impact on entities of the same scale, is to reduce it to a bundle of effects. In this way a house would be transformed into a sort of "Chronic House Syndrome", with no commitment to an underlying house. But this is more Latour than DeLanda, given the latter's fondness for all that is unactualized. The only one of the four criteria that gets at the entity itself, rather than its symptoms, is redundant causation. To say that a given assemblage could have had many different causes is to say that it is *cut off* from its genetic history.

What is important about an assemblage is that is has certain *properties* that make a snake-assemblage more dangerous than a chair-singularity, or an unwritten Shakespeare play a more devastating loss than the failed projects of commercial hacks. The qualities of the thing exceed the part that gave rise to them. But just as importantly, they are deeper than any actualization of them. The fact that a thing has qualities does not mean that they are detected in some way by the environment, but only that the environment *might* detect them if only it were equipped to do so. But if a thing has inherent qualities that it seems to require in order to be what it is, this sounds an awful lot like *essence*. Yet DeLanda avoids this term at all costs. Why?

3. Essence

DeLanda spends little time discussing the Platonic version of essence, apparently not viewing it as a serious threat. It is different with Aristotle, whose three-tiered model of genus, species, and individual is subjected to concerted attack. If there are moments in the 2002 book when DeLanda seems to assign individual entities solely to the actual sphere while reserving the virtual for pre-individual attractors and singularities, this is clearly not the case four years later. As DeLanda concludes: "unlike [Aristotle's] taxonomic essentialism in which genus, species and individual are separate ontological categories, the ontology of assemblages is flat since it contains nothing but different-scaled *individual singularities* (or *haecceities*).... This implies that persons are not the only individual entities involved in social processes, but also individual communities, individual organizations, individual cities and individual nation-states."[92] The important point here is that individual entities are not something that needs to be overcome. Any assemblage of any scale is a real singularity, deeper than its overdetermination in some set of relations to other things. Not only Egyptians are social actors, but also the Zamalek neighborhood, the American University, Cairo itself, and Egypt qua Egypt. All are *haecceities*.

In order to arrive at a flat ontology, then, all three of Aristotle's terms (individual, species, and genus) must be collapsed into individual singularities. DeLanda can easily do this to individuals by making them singularities: namely, by making them never fully actualized; they apparently do not need to sacrifice their individuality. We can do it to species by essentially getting rid of them and replacing them with countless individuals that happen to occupy a closed-off reproductive pool, à la Darwin. But what about the genus?

Here things are different. Whereas species were more or less dismissed as illusory constructs made up of numerous individuals, genera for DeLanda have to be viewed in purely abstract or topological terms:

> The question is, if species can be replaced by individual singularities, can the same be done to genera? The answer is that the highest levels of biological classifications, that of kingdom.... or even phyla –including the phylum 'chordata' to which humans as vertebrate animals belong– need a different treatment. A phylum may be considered an abstract body-plan common to all vertebrates and, as such.... each realization of the body-plan will exhibit a completely different set of metric relations.[93]

Stated differently, "a body-plan defines a space of possibilities.... and this space has a topological structure." Returning to more familiar terrain, DeLanda adds that "the formal study of these possibility spaces is more advanced in physics and chemistry, where they are referred to as 'phase spaces.' Their structure is given by topological invariants called 'attractors,' as well as by.... dimensions that represent the 'degrees of freedom,' or relevant ways of changing, of concrete physical or chemical dynamical systems."[94] Employing a Deleuzian term, DeLanda refers also to "a *diagram*, a set of universal singularities that would be the equivalent of [a] body-plan, or.... that would structure the space of possibilities associated with the assemblage."[95] Outside biology, DeLanda finds an example of such diagrams in Max Weber's schema of *ideal types* of legitimacy in social organization.[96] Sacred, charismatic, and rational/bureaucratic forms of legitimation can be found in numerous different cultural and historical settings, just as vertebrates come in various different forms, some of them utterly monstrous.

But this leads us back to a two-layered world of the kind suggested in 2002 in *Intensive Science and Virtual Philosophy*. For DeLanda now gives us an absolute opposition between *individual* singularities such as dogs, and *universal* singularities such as vertebrates. As he puts it, "we may refer to.... topological invariants as *universal singularities* because they are singular or special topological features that are shared by many different systems."[97] And further, "distributions of these universal singularities.... would replace Aristotle's genera, while individual singularities replace his species."[98] And finally:

> the link from one to another would not be a process of logical differentiation, but one of *historical differentiation*, that is, a process involving the divergent evolution of all the different vertebrate species that realize the abstract body-plan. The taxonomic categories bridging the level of phyla to that of species would represent the successive points of divergence that historically differentiated the body-plan.[99]

Here we have the heart of DeLanda's vision. But I would like to raise three separate objections. First, it is doubtful whether there needs to be any distinction between individual and universal singularities. If no such distinction is needed, we would be left merely with singularities of different scales, not of two vastly different types. Second, the attempt to replace the "essence" of individual singularities with dynamic historico-genetic processes must fail due to the assemblage theory's own principles. And third, the attempt to place universal singularities in a continuum must also fail. What we need is a philosophy closely related to DeLanda's but rather different on certain key points: an ontology of individuals cut off from their histories and cut off just as much from each other.

First, let's consider the supposed difference between universal and individual singularities. What both have in common, we have repeatedly seen, is a richness beyond all specific actualization and beyond all relation with other things, which never fully exhaust them. For DeLanda the dog must always be something more than the dog running or eating, since none of these activities fully exhaust the dog. For an author like Latour, by contrast, the dog is always fully specific in its activities at any given moment, and must be established as the supposed "same" dog by some outside observer who *fabricates* a solid link between each of its fleeting incarnations. Meanwhile, "vertebrate" is supposed to be more universal than the dog simply because it is an abstract body-plan common to rabbits, humans, and the extinct ankylosaurus. One problem is that this violates DeLanda's assertion that the difference between "macro" and "micro" is not absolute, that these two terms "should not be associated with two fixed levels of scale but used to denote the concrete parts and the resulting emergent whole at any given spatial scale."[100] There is no getting off the hook by claiming that universal singularities are non-spatial and hence not bound to DeLanda's axiom of micro/macro interchangeability.

The point is this: a dog may be less universal and more specific than "vertebrate", but "vertebrate" in turn is less universal and more specific than "animal." More generally, it is strange that DeLanda's ontology allows room for individual dogs and also the universal vertebrate, but not for anything like a real species of dog apart from all its individual members. If "dog" consists of countless individual dogs, there is no evident reason why vertebrate should not consist of individual vertebrate animals. In short, it is a bad idea to find *specific* zones of reality that count as individuals and *other* specific zones that count as universals. All we have are individual entities never actualized, as the assemblage theory itself suggests. Behind the running dog is the dog itself, marked by an excess deeper than the overly specific action of running. Behind the dog is not a vertebrate genus, but the components of the dog, each of them deeper and richer than their actualization to form the dog. And these components are haunted in turn by an excess of their own components, in a descending chain of unactualized *individuals* having no evident end point in the tiniest known micro-components of present-day physics. The "micro" and "macro" layers are never fixed.

Second, we must note yet again that DeLanda's attempt to replace the essences of individuals with their dynamic genetic histories is countered by the principle of redundant causation. In a now famous example, he observes that we can accept the periodic table of elements "while refusing to reify its natural kinds. Atoms of a given species would be considered individual entities produced by recurrent processes [of nucleosynthesis] taking place within individual stars. Even though, unlike organisms, these atoms display much less variation, the fact they were born in a concrete process gives each of them a history."[101] But fascinating though it may be to speak of the biography of individual atoms, no biography preserves *all* information about its subject, and not just for reasons of the publisher's budget. As DeLanda himself notes, much information is completely redundant. When speaking of the demographic factors in an election, most personal anecdotes are irrelevant, since different anecdotal incidents would have led to the same result. A machine remains the same even when individual gears and leavers are replaced, and the same is true for a human body and its constituent atoms. Redundant causation means that an assemblage is to some extent autonomous, cut off from the history that engendered it. Only certain historical details remain relevant to the atom, and even these are relevant not *qua* history, but only because they leave some sort of genuine trace in the atom. The fact that hydrogen was formed in one kind of star rather than another is likely irrelevant to its present constitution, since most history is redundant, and reality forgets most of the road by which it arrived where it is today. Memory is obstructed, not infinite. Hence, an entity is always cut off from its dynamic historical genesis and does crystallize in some particular present, even if it withholds itself from full actualization in relation to other things.

In passing, I would like to argue against all attempts to identify figures such as Bergson or DeLanda with a completely different current containing figures such as Latour and Whitehead. Sometimes the phrase "process philosophy" is used loosely to encompass all such figures, who are joined by their rejection of old-fashioned substance and perhaps by little else. Notice that substance is rejected for opposite reasons in these two traditions. For the school of dynamic becoming, the problem with substance is its excessive rigidity and fixity. Substance is always too specific for someone like DeLanda. But for a relational philosopher such as Latour, the problem with substance is its *insufficient* rigidity: it pretends to hide behind all specific determinations and endure through shifting states of affairs, when in fact it should be thoroughly defined by them. If Bergson rejects any isolated instant, the thoroughly relational thought of Latour and Whitehead *requires* entities to be fully articulated in an instant, even if this occasion must immediately perish.

And finally, we should ask whether singularities of any kind can exist in a continuum. For obvious reasons, DeLanda finds continuity more appealing than chunks of fixed, discrete essence: "unlike essences," he says, "which as abstract general entities coexist side by side sharply distinguished from one another, concrete universals must be thought as meshed together in a continuum".[102] The problem is that there can be no *real* continuum if we accept that the real means that which is never fully actualized. Even if we hold that there can be no real without *some* actualization of it (and I would disagree even with this) the whole point of the real for DeLanda is *realism*: the excess of something beyond any actualization or even any sum of actualizations.

In other words, the *real* world, and not just the actual world, is quantized in precisely the manner that Bhaskar imagined. If we say "God created the pigeonholes, and humans invented the spectrum," this inverted cliché is not strictly true either, but it is much closer to the truth than Flew's initial platitude. If Bergson is famous for a model in which the cosmos itself is dynamic movement and humans break it into pieces, DeLanda slides toward the role of an upside-down Bergson, whether deliberately or not. The real world must itself be filled with chunks, and the realm of actualized states of affairs must be where continuum is found. Assemblages do each have an essence, and they are cut off both from their own dynamical-genetic history and from their neighboring entities as well.

But this leads to an obvious problem. If real individuals are defined by their thoroughly non-relational or trans-relational character, then how can they relate to anything else at all? How is causation possible? This problem was raised earlier by two different sorts of philosophies: first by the Islamic and French occasionalists, who reserved for God not only the power of creation, but the power of any causal relation at all. Second, the problem was raised by Hume, who is known to have been a great admirer of the great French occasionalist Malebranche. Ironically, Hume's approach to occasionalism is merely the inverted one, with the human mind playing the role of God such that *only* the mind links things through habit. In both cases, one privileged entity is allowed a magical transgression beyond the ban that radical realism places on relationality. Whereas occasionalism accepts the existence of autonomous substances and has trouble relating them, Hume begins with their relations and can find no way to establish their autonomous life beyond their relations in and to the mind.

In other words, both Hume and the occasionalists solve the problem of relation with a somewhat hypocritical appeal to a magical super-entity (whether *deus ex machina* or *mens ex machina*) that is somehow able to enter relations even though nothing else can. Neither option can work in a DeLandian sort of realism, since the mind for DeLanda is never a necessary ingredient in any interaction, and God does not appear in his philosophy at all. Hence, what DeLanda needs is a sort of "local occasionalism" in which entities are somehow equipped for mutual interaction despite their non-relational character.

4. Causation

In his 2006 book *A New Philosophy of Society*, DeLanda draws a distinction between linear causation on the one hand and catalysis on the other. Linear causation means just what it suggests: the same cause leads to the same effect every time. By contrast, catalysts merely encourage certain reactions rather than automatically entailing them: a cigarette, for instance, merely *catalyzes* lung cancer, since not all smokers will become cancer patients and not all such patients were smokers. In addition, DeLanda says that linear causation is usually *material* while catalysis is normally *expressive*. This contrast is interesting. The "material" realm for DeLanda generally refers to the functional infrastructure of a thing, such as gas and sewer lines for a city. The "expressive" zone of the world refers to the excessive, non-functional surface of a thing: a city's skyline, for instance. The skyline proudly announces the city in the same way that a face announces a character; both could be altered or damaged without affecting the underlying functionality of the city or person wounded thereby.

Now, if entities are catalysts rather than causes for DeLanda, this is similar to Bhaskar's vision (derived ultimately from John Stuart Mill) of multiple causal factors in every situation. For instance: an explosion may have a lit match as its proximate cause, but other causal agents include the gunpowder it ignites, the unusually dry October that made the warehouse vulnerable to fire, and the drunken state of the night watchman who let the saboteur creep through without detection. A vast array of entities participates in the cause of any event, which makes them resemble DeLandian catalysts. In the eyes of Bhaskar, this is enough to overturn determinisim, since no one cause can be held responsible for any event. Similarly, DeLanda thinks catalysis is enough to put an end to linear causation. But this is clearly incorrect. The multiplicity of causes merely complicates our *analysis* of the causal conditions. By no means does it establish that the relative impotence of each individual cause adds up to indeterminacy or free will as the ultimate result. In other words, though a cigarette may not yield the same result every time, this dodges the real question. That question is whether the same cigarette *plus* the same genetics *plus* the the same diet *plus* the same environment, etc. will yield the same result every time. In this sense, DeLanda's catalysis does not escape the mechanical nature of linear causation.

But in another sense he does not allow for linear causation at all, since he calls it "material". If we take the material to refer to the intrinsic reality of an assemblage apart from its outer expressive effects, then in some sense the material must recede from any actualization, and indeed any relation at all. As a result, it seems that all causal relation must occur on the *expressive* level: that is to say, on the *inessential* level where the properties of an assemblage are not concealed and non-actualized, but manifest and fully actualized. This finds support in what we already know about causal relations: namely, that the essential features of a thing are destroyed by way of its accidental ones. The greatness of Lincoln is destroyed by a small piece of lead penetrating the man's skin; a Picasso portrait of Dora Maar might someday be ruined by a spilt glass of orange juice. It is also supported by aesthetics, where it has been noted that metaphors work best when they link two entities through *inessential* features. "A pen is like a pencil" has no metaphorical effect, whereas "a pen is like a viper" does, despite the purely peripheral link of their vaguely similar physical form. And finally it finds support in ethics, in the remark by Emmanuel Levinas that violence is an attempt to possess what is strong in someone through what is weak in them (the Lincoln assassination, again).

In short, the expressive surface of the world or zone of mere accidents is the only site where relations can take place. Deleuze had noted that expression can take on a causal role, and DeLanda had already applauded this point, but without sensing that perhaps *only* the expressive realm can be causal. Yet expression does not occur on a surface; there really is no surface in this sense. To think that the world has a surface is to commit oneself to the old two-layered model in which a real unactu-alized world-in-the-depths is doubled up by an actualized world-on-the-surface. Instead of this, DeLanda's model has given us a series of assemblages linked in an ascending and descending chain. This means that the only place where any relation between two assemblages can occur is on the *inside* of a larger assemblage. And since assemblages are quantized into chunks rather than bleeding into a continuum, their interiors will automatically be cut off from the insides of other assemblages.

This claim is less of an oddity than it might initially seem. A similar point was already made by Edmund Husserl in the *Logical Investigations* when he claimed that intentionality is both one and two. If someone perceives a tree, the relation between the perceiver and the tree is actually a new assemblage. They come into contact in such a way as to form a new entity, and the interior of this entity is the place where the real perceiver confronts an actualized phantom or figment of the concealed real object that is perceived. Note that the same is true in reverse: if the object confronts me, the real object is confronting a sort of phantasmal image of me on the interior of a similar but inverted object. A certain form of panpyschism is the obvious result.

But what also results is a new awareness of how relations always entail the creation of a new assemblage, even if a temporary one. If two jets collide in mid-air and fly away burning, we normally think of this situation in terms of mutual qualitative effects on two independent entities. A better analysis, in DeLandian terms, would be that the two jets briefly formed a new entity, which damaged both of them through that power of assemblages that we already encountered as "retroactive effect on their parts." They then decomposed into separate entities again, this time fully aflame. In other words causation primarily means creating a new object, not creating new effects on pre-existent objects. The two flaming jets, spiraling to their doom, are more the symptoms of causation than the embodiments of it.

But what about the theme of this conference: The Open? I choose to interpret this topic in terms of the openness of the future. Are future events in some way predetermined, or is every-thing left open? In one sense, it seems that the creation of new assemblages will always be possible, and hence novelty can emerge. Insofar as causation happens in the expressive realm, it occurs within the zone where the *accidental* features of a thing unfold. However, neither Bhaskar nor DeLanda solve the problem of freedom with their colorful mist of catalysts and multiple causal factors. The complexity of such factors may lie beyond our own understanding, but perhaps not beyond that of a deity or a malevolent supercomputer. Some new approach is needed to find openness amidst the turmoil of linear causes.

11. Objects, Matter, Sleep, and Death (2009)

This piece was originally a lecture given in Toulouse, France on 18 November, 2008 at a conference on non-anthropological subjectivity. My fellow Speculative Realist Quentin Meillassoux was also among the speakers. At that time the following lecture was entitled "Intentional Objects for Non-Humans". But while preparing for a June 2009 conference on materialism in Zagreb, Croatia, I was asked by Professor Nathan Brown to submit a short unpublished essay for advance distribution to conference attendees, and the Toulouse lecture was selected for that purpose. The following is the shortened and retitled Zagreb version of the essay.

If we define "object" as that which has a unified and autonomous life apart from its relations, accidents, qualities, and moments, it is obvious that objects remain unpopular in philosophy today. To some they sound a bit too much like old-fashioned substances, and in our time everyone is united in cursing and whipping those substances:

*Quentin Meillassoux has given a brilliant analysis, in *After Finitude*, of the "correlationist" attitude in philosophy. The correlationist thinks that there is no human without world, nor world without human, but only a primal correlation or rapport between the two. Hence, the object has no autonomy for the correlationist. In franker terms, the object does not exist.

*For the empiricist, there is also no object, since there are only bundles of discrete qualities. The unified object is a fiction produced by customary conjunction in the habits of the human mind. There are no objects for empiricism.

*What about materialists? They might seem to be the most object-friendly of all thinkers. But in fact they are not. On the contrary, materialists are generally reducers. They start their work by exterminating all large- and medium-sized entities, and ultimately find reality only in physical microparticles such as quarks and electrons, and possibly more exotic ones called strings. And even if one or more of these particles turns out to be the final layer of the cosmos, it will still not give us the reality we need. As Bertrand Russell admits in *The Analysis of Matter*, the entities of physics are purely relational. They give us spatio-temporal co-ordinates and tangible properties that can be measured, but all these features have meaning only in *relation* to other things. What does the relating? It would be autonomous *objects* that do the relating. But there are no objects in materialism.

*Bruno Latour provides the most democratic philosophy of actors that one could imagine. Ignoring the old distinction between substance and aggregate, he says that electrons, humans, tigers, apricots, armies, square circles, and bald kings of France are all *actors* to an equal degree. This is very close to an object-oriented philosophy. But rather than give objects their full independence, he defines them in terms of their relations. As he puts it, an actor is no more than what it "transforms, modifies, perturbs, or creates". An actor is what an actor does. But if objects are autonomous, then they must be more than actors. Hence there are no objects in Latour's actor-network theory, at least not the kind we are looking for.

*Finally, it is popular these days to say that the world is a continuum, a primal dynamic flux broken into pieces only by the needs of human praxis or by functional relations of some other sort. I do not agree, but hold instead that the world itself is *quantized* or broken into discrete chunks, even if they are stranger chunks than the old-fashioned substances of yesterday. To see this, let's look briefly at a philosopher who has nothing to do with panpyschism at all: Martin Heidegger.

1. All Relations are on the Same Footing

Heidegger is most famous for asking the question of the meaning of being. His admirers seem to think this question is deeper than any specific answer, while his enemies hold the question to be so vague and empty that no progress can ever be made. Both are wrong. Heidegger *does* answer the question of the meaning of being, with his famous tool-analysis in *Being and Time*. The story is so well known that there is no reason to repeat it in detail. While Husserl's phenomenology describes things in terms of their appearance to consciousness, Heidegger notes that things primarily *do not* appear in consciousness. Instead, they withdraw from view into invisible usefulness. The floor in this room, the oxygen in the air, the heart and kidneys that keep us alive, are generally hidden unless and until they malfunction.

In the usual, lazy misreading, this is enough to make Heidegger a "pragmatist". Invisible background practice comes first; visible conscious and theoretical awareness comes later. But this interpretation is superficial. For it is not really a question of visibility and invisibility for humans, but of the transformation of a thing's reality. When I look at or theorize about a hammer, oxygen, floor, or bodily organs, my access to these things is a mere caricature. It oversimplifies the dark and concealed reality of these objects themselves, and gives at best a *partial* description of the subterranean hammer whose properties can never be exhaustively known. However, human *praxis* does exactly the same thing! By using the hammer, I have no more direct access to it than when I think about it or look at it. On the contrary, praxis is even *more* stupid than theory, distorting and oversimplifying the reality of a thing even more than theory does. Heidegger is no pragmatist.

Yet there is a further step that Heidegger never took, though he ought to have done so, and it builds an unexpected road from his philosophy to a kind of panpyschist position. If theory and praxis both distort, caricature, or transform the hidden reality of things, then the same must be true of any relation whatever. When fire burns cotton, does it have access to the color or smell that we humans are able to detect in it? Inanimate objects do not make direct contact with one another any more than we do with them. The distortions that arise from relation are not a special burden or flaw of the human or animal psyche, but spring from relationality in general. Inanimate objects are perhaps even more ruthless than we are in reducing the richness of things to a small number of traits.

In other words, *all relations are on the same footing*. This strikes at the central problem of philosophy since Kant. That problem does not lie in the endless dispute over whether there are real things-in-themselves beyond human access. No, the problem is that whether one believes in the *Ding an sich* or not, in either case it is this sole gap or non-gap between human and world that is taken to be fundamental. One of Latour's great achievements is to save us from this predicament by allowing that the relation between paint and a house, or rain and desert sand, are negotiations or translations no less than the relations between a scientist and the world. In any case, we now find a global dualism between the reality of objects and their more or less distorted or translated images for other objects. Human theory and praxis are closely associated with the latter half of this dualism, and this already brings us to the verge of panpsychism. Either psyche extends down into the lowest regions of being, or else psyche as we know it is built out of something more primitive.

2. Intentional Objects

In establishing a region of tool-being deeper than all human access, Heidegger criticized his teacher Husserl for reducing the world to its purely phenomenal character. The point is fair enough, but misses what is most important about Husserl. Namely, Husserl's most important discovery is the *intentional* object. Even in the claustrophobic phenomenal world he creates, an amazing drama unfolds between objects and their qualities. Indeed, perhaps only *because* of Husserl's imprisonment in the narrow phenomenal sphere does he feel the desperate need to look for a new fissure or rift in this sphere itself.

Franz Brentano revived the medieval discussion of intentionality and gave it this form: every mental act has an object, whether it be thinking, wishing, judging, or cases of love and hate. All of these are directed toward some object immanent in the mind. Initially there was no attempt to address the question of the status of objects *outside* the mind. This theme was raised by Brentano's brilliant Polish student Kazimierz Twardowski, who draws a distinction between the *object* outside the mind and the *content* through which it appears immanently within the mind.[103] By doing so he awakened the thinking of the young Husserl, who viewed Twardowksi as both an inspiration and a rival throughout the 1890s, referring to him sometimes with admiration and at other times with misleading contempt.

Everyone usually focuses on just *one* result of Husserl's engagement with Twardowski. Namely, Husserl rejects Twadowski's objects of the outer world and veers more and more toward his well-known idealistic retreat within the phenomenological sphere. But this is only half the story, and not the most interesting half. While it is true that Husserl stays within the phenomenal kingdom, he also preserves the object: he simply places both object and content *within the phenomenal sphere*. In other words, Husserl creates a new dualism of intentional object and intentional content. And this has surprising consequences for metaphysics.

Insofar as empiricism thinks that objects are just bundles of qualities, Husserl is the anti-empiricist par excellence. I always see a tree from a certain angle and distance, at a certain time of day, in some utterly specific mood. Yet all of these details are overdeterminations of the tree. The tree as an *intentional* object is not a real object growing and nourishing itself in the outer world, but neither is it reducible to the exact details through which it is given at any moment to consciousness. While the real tree is always something *more* than whatever I see of it, the intentional tree is always something *less*. That is to say, I always see it much too specifically, encrusted with too much accidental color or from an accidental angle, or in some purely coincidental melancholic mood. Any of these details could be changed without changing the intentional tree, which always remains an enduring *unit* for as long as I recognize it as one. This is the meaning of an intentional object. It is not an empty *je ne sais quoi* projected onto unformed sense data, because in fact it precedes and shapes any such data. As Merleau-Ponty knew, the black of a pen and of an executioner's hood are different even if their wavelength of light is exactly the same. The qualities are *impregnated* with the objects to which they are attached

Along with the Heideggerian difference between the reality of things and their phenomenal apparitions, we have a new dualism *within* the phenomena, between unified phenomenal objects and their specific content. This is not some special tragic feature of human or animal psychology. Instead, any intentional relation (and we have already seen that such relation is ubiquitous) will be equally haunted by a split between intentional objects and the accidentally specific ways in which they appear. There is no time here to establish this point in detail. But perhaps it is enough to see that objects may register numerous changes in their environment without those changes being *decisive*. The cotton can become five degrees hotter, but until the critical point is reached where it bursts into flame, it is still cotton rather than burning cotton.

3. On the Inside

Now, let's consider another famous feature found in all intentionality: "immanent objectivity". According to Brentano, the object of any mental act is immanent in the mind, not really present in the outer world. But this shows a certain lack of imagination. After all, why should immanent objects be immanent *in the mind*? A different option turns out to provide the true answer.

Husserl remarks that there is a certain paradox about intentionality, insofar as it is both one and two. On the one hand my relation to the tree is a single unified whole. I can reflect upon it later as one thing, and other people can reflect upon it as well, if for some unknown reason they should choose to analyze my psychic life. In fact my relation with the tree is a new object in its own right, even if it does not endure for long and consists of no physical matter. I call it an *object* because it is a unified reality not exhausted by any relation to it from the outside. But at the same time intentionality is also two, not just one. For I never fuse homogeneously into the tree in a blinding flash of light. The tree always remains separate from me, standing over against me. Moreover, this twofold is also *asymmetrical,* since here the *real* me encounters a merely *phenomenal* or *intentional* tree. When by contrast the real tree encounters the phenomenal caricature of me, as it must in all cases when it comes into contact with me, this must result in a different but closely related object. And we now see that such spaces are always found on the *interior* of another object. The twofold intentional relation between me and the tree is located *inside* the unified object that the tree and I form. It is the hollow, molten, inner core of objects where all intentional relation occurs. Against the usual model of human intelligence as a critical, transcendent, liberated force, the mind is more like a burrowing animal digging deeper, laterally, or upward through the interiors of things.

Furthermore, the view stated earlier that no two things can touch directly is reminiscent of two moments in the history of philosophy. First, the Islamic and French *occasionalists* held that no two things are able to touch except through God. Second, Humean *skepticism* held that no two things are linked except through the habits or customary conjunctions linked in the mind. What both positions have in common is a basic hypocrisy. While saying that nothing is truly linked to anything else, these positions invoke a *deus ex machina* or *mens ex machina* that will form an exception to the rule. One privileged entity is allowed to form links where others cannot. Against this notion, I propose the more democratic solution of a local occasionalism, in which every entity that exists must somehow be equipped to serve as a medium of contact between two others. And as we have seen, the one place where two objects can always touch is on the *interior* of another. It is here that the causal mechanisms of the world must unfold.

4. Polypsychism, Not Panpsychism

All of this might sound like a strange panpsychist alternative to the scientific world-view. But what is most remarkable is the way in which it sets a *limit* to panpsychism. The panpsychist view, namely, is that anything that exists must also perceive. But the view I have suggested is that anything that *relates* must perceive. Only by becoming a piece of a larger object, only by entering the interior of a larger one, does an entity have anything like a psyche. This means that entities have psyches accidentally rather than in their own right. For our model allows for entities to exist apart from all relations. This makes it not just conceivable, but also necessary, that there be entities at any moment that are at the very top of their chains of parts while relating to nothing further. For various reasons it is good to think of an infinite regress downward in the world, with no tiniest layer of material microparticle bringing an end to the chain of beings. But the same does not hold in reverse. The idea of a 'universe as a whole' actually seems like a fruitless abstraction, and there is some autonomy for the various different parts of the cosmos, all of which require *work* to be interwoven together, which proves that they are not already interwoven. Imagine an ocean without a bottom, but with a turbulent surface where certain drops of water have neighbors below but none above. This model of the world is what results from our previous discussion. The name for an object that exists without relating, exists without perceiving, is a *sleeping* entity: or a *dormant* object, to use the lovely term our language has stolen from the French. Dormant objects are real, but currently without psyche.

Each night we sleep, making ourselves as dormant as we can, stripping away the accidental accretions of the day and gathering ourselves once more in the essential life where we are untouched by external relations. Death, by contrast, is nothing like sleep. Death is a subversion from below, a corruption by means of failing parts, when vital components fail in such a way that they can no longer be refreshed or replaced.

Notes

1   Martin Heidegger, "Einblick in das was ist." In *Bremer und Freiburger Vorträge*. (Frankfurt: Vittorio Klostermann, 1994.)

2   Graham Harman, *Tool-Being: Heidegger and the Metaphysics of Objects*. (Chicago: Open Court, 2002.)

3   Martin Heidegger, *The Fundamental Concepts of Metaphysics: World, Finitude, Solitude*. Transl. W. McNeill and N. Walker. (Bloomington, IN: Indiana Univ. Press, 2001.)

4   Martin Heidegger, *Phänomenologie des religiösen Lebens*, p. 113. (Frankfurt, Vittorio Klostermann, 1995.)

5   Alphonso Lingis, *The Community of Those Who Have Nothing in Common*, p. 25. (Bloomington, IN: Indiana Univ. Press., 1994.)

6   Ibid., p. 23.

7   Ibid., p. 42.

8   Ibid., pp. 42-43.

9   Ibid., p. 45.

10   Alphonso Lingis, *Foreign Bodies*, p. 17. (London: Routledge, 1994.)

11   Ibid., p. 32.

12   Ibid., p. 44.

13   *The Community of Those Who Have Nothing in Common*, p. 49.

14   Ibid., p. 50.

15   Ibid., p. 45.

16   *Foreign Bodies*, p. 18.

17   Ibid., p. 24.

18   The reference is to Jean Baudrillard, a favorite author of mine during the early 1990s.

19   Charles Hartshorne, *Whitehead's Philosophy: Selected Essays, 1935-1970*, p. 15. (Lincoln, NE: Univ. of Nebraska Press, 1972.)

20   Sokal's article was published in *Social Text*, 46/47 (Spring/Summer 1996), pp. 217-252.

21 The supposed gathering was a fiction, invoked in my lecture only for the rhetorical purposes of entertainment.

22 Alan Sokal and Jean Bricmont, *Fashionable Nonsense: Postmodern Intellectuals' Abuse of Science.* (New York: Picador, 1999.)

23 The reference is to Gallagher's Grill and Tavern, the usual post-lecture gathering place of DePaul students and faculty in those days.

24 This prediction was obviously far too optimistic.

25 Latour lectured at Northwestern University in the Chicago suburb of Evanston in May 1998. I did not speak with him on that occasion, despite the odd coincidence of flying from Chicago to Paris a few days later on the same plane as Latour himself. He was simply returning home; I was going there as a tourist to celebrate my thirtieth birthday.

26 Bruno Latour, *We Have Never Been Modern*, p. 1. Transl. by Catherine Porter. (Cambridge, MA: Harvard University Press, 1993.)

27 Ibid., p. 2.

28 The reference is to the NATO bombing of Serbia during the 1999 Kosovo crisis, still underway at the time of this lecture.

29 *We Have Never Been Modern.*, p. 4.

30 Ibid.

31 Ibid.

32 Ibid., p. 5.

33 Ibid.

34 Ibid.

35 Richard Rorty, *Truth and Progress: Philosophical Papers, Volume 3*, p. 8. (Cambridg, UK: Cambridge University Press, 1998.)

36 Graham Harman, letter to Richard Rorty of 8 November 1998.

37 Richard Rorty, personal communication, 16 November 1998. (Despite Rorty's polite salutation, I was not yet a professor but still a doctoral candidate.)

38   Latour, *We Have Never Been Modern*, pp. 6-7.

39   Ibid., p. 37.

40   Ibid., p. 51.

41   Bruno Latour, "Les objets ont-ils une histoire? Rencontre de Pasteur et de Whitehead dans un bain d'acide lacticque." In Isabelle Stengers (ed.), *L'effet Whitehead*. (Paris: Flammarion, 1994.)

42   Latour, *We Have Never Been Modern*, pp. 49-50.

43   Ibid., pp. 51-52.

44   Ibid., pp. 52-53.

45   Ibid., pp. 53-54.

46   Ibid., pp. 54-55.

47   Ibid., pp. 56-57.

48   The reference is to the upcoming annual DePaul graduate student philosophy conference, held in May 1999 under the title "Philosophy at the Ends of Centuries," where I spoke on Giordano Bruno.

49   *We Have Never Been Modern.*, p. 60.

50   Ibid., p. 61.

51   Ibid.

52   Ibid., pp. 64-65.

53   Ibid., p. 65.

54   Ibid., pp. 65-66.

55   Ibid., p. 66.

56   Ibid., p. 128.

57   In fact, 2002 was the first year when such positions were first introduced into continental philosophy, both in my own *Tool-Being* and in Manuel DeLanda's *Intensive Science and Virtual Philosophy*. (London: Continuum, 2002.)

58   This was first pointed out to me in 1991 by Alphonso Lingis in a very helpful set of comments on my paper for the Master's Degree at Penn State University. He cited Levinas as the inspiration for his idea.

59 Steven Nadler. "'No Necessary Connection': The Medieval Roots of the Occasionalist Roots of Hume." In *The Monist* 79 (1996), pp. 448-466.

60 Only a few months later, the Husserlian term "eidos" was adopted to fill this role.

61 See especially Manuel DeLanda, *A New Philosophy of Society* (London: Continuum, 2006).

62 *Intensive Science and Virtual Philosophy*, p. 4.

63 *A New Philosophy of Society*, p. 4.

64 Ibid., p. 1. Emphasis added.

65 *Intensive Science and Virtual Philosophy*, p. 29.

66 Ibid., p. 35. Emphasis added.

67 Deleuze, *Difference and Repetition*, pp. 208-209. As cited on pp. 30-31 of DeLanda, *Intensive Science and Virtual Philosophy*.

68 *Intensive Science and Virtual Philosophy*, p. 30. Emphasis removed.

69 Bruno Latour, *Pandora's Hope*, p. 122.

70 Ibid., p. 35.

71 Ibid., p. 21. Italics removed.

72 *Intensive Science and Virtual Philosophy*, pp. 83, 84.

73 Ibid., p. 40.

74 Bhaskar, *A Realist Theory of Science*, p. 13. (London: Verso, 1997.)

75 Ibid., p. 64.

76 Ibid., p. 17.

77 Ibid., p. 32.

78 Ibid., p. 67.

79 *A New Philosophy of Society*, p. 28.

80 *A Realist Theory of Science*, p. 59.

81 Ibid., p. 113.

82 Ibid., p. 59.

83 Ibid., p. 171.

84 Cited ibid., p. 213.

85 Ibid.

86   *A New Philosophy of Society*, p. 4.
87   Ibid., p. 5.
88   Ibid., pp. 34-35.
89   Ibid., p. 37.
90   Ibid., p. 38.
91   Ibid., p. 39.
92   Ibid., p. 28.
93   Ibid., pp. 28-29.
94   Ibid., p. 29.
95   Ibid., p. 30.
96   Ibid.
97   Ibid., p. 29.
98   Ibid.
99   Ibid., pp. 29-30.
100 Ibid., p. 32. Emphasis removed.
101 Ibid., p. 28.
102 Ibid., p. 21. Emphasis removed.
103 Kasimir Twardowski, *On the Content and Object of Presentations*. Transl. by Reinhard Grossmann. (The Hague: Martinus Nijhoff, 1977.)

Contemporary culture has eliminated both the concept of the public and the figure of the intellectual. Former public spaces – both physical and cultural – are now either derelict or colonized by advertising. A cretinous anti-intellectualism presides, cheerled by expensively educated hacks in the pay of multinational corporations who reassure their bored readers that there is no need to rouse themselves from their interpassive stupor. The informal censorship internalized and propagated by the cultural workers of late capitalism generates a banal conformity that the propaganda chiefs of Stalinism could only ever have dreamt of imposing. Zer0 Books knows that another kind of discourse – intellectual without being academic, popular without being populist – is not only possible: it is already flourishing, in the regions beyond the striplit malls of so-called mass media and the neurotically bureaucratic halls of the academy. Zer0 is committed to the idea of publishing as a making public of the intellectual. It is convinced that in the unthinking, blandly consensual culture in which we live, critical and engaged theoretical reflection is more important than ever before.